The MYSTERY FANcier

Vol. 3, No. 3
May/June
1979

THE MYSTERY FANCIER

Volume 3 Number 3
May/June 1979

TABLE OF CONTENTS

```
MYSTERIOUSLY SPEAKING. . . . . . . . . . . . . . . . . .  1
Introducing Alexandra Roudybush, by Gerie Frazier. . . .  2
Three Gentle Men, by Mary Jean DeMarr. . . . . . . . . .  5
The Investigation: Fiction and Fact, by Jo Ann Vicarel . 15
IT'S ABOUT CRIME, by Marvin Lachman. . . . . . . . . . . 17
The Books of Geoffrey Homes, by Ted Dukeshire. . . . . . 19
The Nero Wolfe Saga, Part XIII, by Guy M. Townsend . . . 22
MYSTERY*FILE: Short Reviews by Steve Lewis . . . . . . . 31
VERDICTS (More Reviews). . . . . . . . . . . . . . . . . 40
THE DOCUMENTS IN THE CASE (Letters). . . . . . . . . . . 50
```

The MYSTERY FANcier
(USPS:428-590)
is edited and published bi-monthly by Guy M. Townsend, 1120 Bluebird Lane, Memphis, Tennessee 38116, U.S.A. Contributions of all descriptions are welcomed. Deadline for the July/August 1979 issue: 15 July 1979.

SUBSCRIPTION RATES: Domestic second class mail, $9.00 per year (6 issues); Overseas surface mail, $9.00; Overseas airmail, $12.00. Overseas subscribers please pay in international money order, check drawn on U.S. bank, or currency; no checks drawn on foreign banks, please. Make checks payable to Guy M. Townsend, not *The MYSTERY FANcier*.

Second class postage paid at Memphis, Tennessee

Copyright 1979 by Guy M. Townsend
All rights reserved for contributors
ISSN:0146-3160

MYSTERIOUSLY SPEAKING . . .

This is the last issue of TMF to come from the Bluebird Lane address. Actually, I have already moved to Blytheville, Arkansas (1325 West Hearn St., zip 72315), and have acquired a new post office address in Osceola, Arkansas (Box 879, zip 72370), but this issue is going out on my old second class permit while the post office is busy processing a new one for the new address. The reason for this latest address change-- my fifth since starting this magazine--is personal, but I see no reason to make a secret of it: my wife and I are getting a divorce. No condolences are in order; the marriage was a bad idea (her's) anyway, and never really worked, so when she decided she wanted out I was delighted to accommodate her. And that's enough said about that. I would not have mentioned it at all except to explain the latest move and to save myself the time and trouble of having to explain to a number of you in individual letters.

This issue is horribly late, and for that I do apologize. In my defense I can only plead that the pressures of moving, working on the Stout Bibliography and other genre projects, teaching a course in the evening division of the local college (yes, masochist that I am, I have taken that on again), performing the duties of my daytime occupation, and travelling back and forth to visit the kids every week or two, have left me with little time for TMF. My newspaper reviews have dried up to a mere trickle, and I even missed a mailing of DAPA-EM, thereby ruining a perfect record and toppling myself from the top of a statistical hierarchy which Jeff Smith maintains to mystify even the initiates. But, I'm about to find my stride again, and with any luck should be able to get TMF back on schedule within the next couple of issues. *(There's that damned echo again, Martha!)*

I have threatened from time to time to punish those of you who send in sloppy copy by publishing what you send in exactly as you send it in. Well, I decided to do it with this issue, so I began typing the copy as is, warts and all. But you tricky scoundrels must must have anticipated me, because the grammatical errors and misspellings and such were much fewer than usual--so much so, in fact, that I am embarrassed that I even tried it. But not so embarrassed that I'll type this bloody thing over again. Anyway, I'd sure appreciate it if you all will keep up the good work. (And some of you could still do with a little practice.)

This cover, assuming that the printer doesn't bitch it up, is, I'm sure you will agree, superb. The drawing of THE bird is by Karl Cerasoli, who was coaxed into doing it by Carl Larsen. Ain't it beautiful?

I don't think I ever explained about the two "March/April" issues of TMF.

As for the missing page numbers in the last issue, the printer did it.

I am going to confine my remarks to this one page, so as to make room for Marv Lachman's column which has just arrived (don't you just hate folks that won't make deadlines?).

Until next time, I will leave you with this thought:

INTRODUCING ALEXANDRA ROUDYBUSH

By Gerie Frazier

Many months ago a letter to TMF mentioned a shortage of reviews of books written by women. Another subscriber requested reviews of books worth reading, but not very well known. This is an attempt to fulfill both requests.

Alexandra Roudybush (nee Brown) is an American who has lived, quite literally, all over the world. Her father was a foreign newspaper correspondent and her husband, Franklin, was in the diplomatic service. They now live in Paris. I have been unable to find, locally, a complete list of her books but those available to me were written between 1965 and 1975. Currently there is only one book (*The Female of the Species*) still in print, so the library will be the best source for anyone interested in this author.

Mrs. Roudybush, in my opinion, excels at plot development and delineation of characters. Her forte is mystery and suspense rather than the murder mystery per se. Her writing is witty (humerous at times) and always good reading. When murder is done, it is not described in gory detail; when she tosses in a "sex scene" it is not overly explicit; she does not use four-letter language. Whether readers will, or will not, enjoy her books is a matter of one's personal taste in fiction.

The following short reviews are an attempt to "whet the appetite" of those unfamiliar with her writing while not giving away too much of the plot--not an easy thing to do with this author.

Before the Ball Was Over (Doubleday/Crime Club, 1965; 190 pp.). Mrs. Phineas Ashburner (Jeannine, early 50's with a 96 year old semi-invalid husband) and Mrs. Reuben Tor are engaged in a bitter struggle to attain title as the "leading Washington hostess". Mr. Ashburner is enormously wealthy; Mr. Tor is the president of a large corporation. The maneuverings of the ladies is merely the time of the iceberg as sub-plots emerge, including dope smuggling and a proposed jewel theft; with two murders along the way.

Colonel Bruce Henderson, formerly of the U.S. Marines, now Chief of Police in the Capital, is a reluctant guest in the party circuit before being drawn into an investigation in his official capacity. The story is highly entertaining, the characters are nearly to real to be fiction and, in the end, everyone has gotten what they have coming to them--happily the "good guys" as well as the bad.

Death of a Moral Person (Doubleday/Crime Club, 1967; 215 pp.). W. Kirkwood Entwhistle, an unmoral person, has by dastardly means become the president of entwhistle Group Organization. His plans to expand EGO, mainly in France, and the resistance of the board of directors comprise the central plot. The firm of Williamson & Jones, under the influence of Bill Kirchwald, is quietly buying stock of EGO to attempt a take-over. Bill, it develops, is Entwhistle's son and was removed from his father's life by his disillusioned mother (with excellent cause) a few months after his birth. Crime, business and personal intrigue, and two rather sordid deaths are involved.

This story was placed in the category of "Something different"--that it is! It is skillfully written, but it simply did not appeal to me as much as Mrs. Roudybush's other books. I am mystified as to the origin of the book's title. Possibly it is a direct quotation from some other source (page 204) and the suitability of it eludes me.

A Capital Crime (Doubleday/Crime Club, 1969; 192 pp.). Famous newspaper and TV commentator Theodulus Suttler finds the still warm body of Sidonie Lane with whom he has a highly profitable relationship, but does not notify the police. When the corpse is found, chief of police Bruce Henderson and Per Peterson of homicide find the murder investigation leading them into a web of crime and intrigue. Theo Suttler is blackmailed by one woman and coerced by another, both with matrimony in mind. There is much more to come, including another murder, a kidnapping (the victim's death being thwarted by a very percocious child) and romance. Very good reading. Along with mystery and suspense, the author gives a tongue-in-cheek portrayal of "behind the scenes" Washington, D.C.

The House of the Cat (Doubleday/Crime Club, 1970; 191 pp.). A delightful story of suspense and intrigue set in Paris. The main characters are "Madame Zed" (a refreshing change from "X"); the man she loved, lost, and regained; Jason Whitaker who is the super-rich First Secretary at the American Embassy; and Doanda Craig, a young and beautiful American with a mind of her own.

Carefully interwoven plots involve the "House", Jason's lavish entertaining, and the hijacking of a shipment of gold; with the flash-back technique used to develop the main characters. Excellent reading.

A Gastronomic Murder (Doubleday/Crime Club, 1973; 185 pp.). Major George Zillitch of the Quartermaster Corps. with the connivance of his WAC assistant Edna Mae Jones, is busily ripping off uninventoried goodies from palatial homes in occupied Germany while preparing the premises to be residing places for U.S. Military brass. At the Schloss Altberg he accidentally discovers a hidden safe containing exquisite jewels, chessmen set in pearls and dark rubies and other items. Taking the most marketable pieces, George arranges not to have to share this treasure with Edna Mae, secures his release from the Army and disappears. In time he resurfaces in Paris as George Simpson.

Ariane Quatsous, an orphan befriended from an early age by a nurse, Leonie Lafauve (much older and very domineering) has a small winning ticket in the national lottery. Being weary of her job and home life she uses a portion of her winnings to secure the services of "Madame Solange--Marriages Arranged". Soon she is introduced to a likely prospect for matrimony, an American named George Simpson.

Zillitch/Simpson has always appreciated excellent food; Leonie is a self-taught gourmet cook. After the marriage, the Simpson's and Leonie establish a hotel and restaurant which becomes highly successful. This idyllic life slowly disintegrates as jealousy rears it's ugly head, and with the appearance of Ken McCabe a former narcotics agent attempting to locate George Zillitch and the missing loot.

Plenty of suspense, two murders. In a Postscript, Mrs. Roudybush shares a few of the recipes for gourmet foods mentioned in the book. I recommend this one highly.

Suddenly, in Paris (Doubleday/Crime Club, 1975; 162 pp.). Best selling author, Frederick Stone, finds his talent drying up and his money running short. His solution to these problems brings disaster upon him rather than surcease. On his trail is his stepson (the Count of Thross) and Sym Gilkerson, a "security management adviser"--the current euphemism for a private eye. Sym, incidentally, is QUITE a character. Most of the action is in Paris, with a fine climax set in Haiti. To say more, would necessarily give away too much of the plot. Try it--you will probably like it.

THREE GENTLE MEN:
DORIS MILES DISNEY'S CONTINUING DETECTIVES
By Mary Jean DeMarr

Doris Miles Disney (1907-1976) was often praised by reviewers for experimenting, for not repeating herself from novel to novel. Her 49 novels include straight detective stories, inverted mysteries, and combinations of these two forms; comic novels and novels of suspense; studies of character and mood pieces; novels which comment on the contemporary scene, stories set in the past, and some which combine past and present. But characterization is always important, and motivations are carefully handled and credible. Only a few of her novels make use of continuing detectives; readers who became familiar with her craftsmanship did not need the lure of a familiar character to attract them to a new Disney novel. Nevertheless, she did create three continuing detectives, who appear in a number of her most popular novels and who are carefully distinguished from each other, both professionally and personally.

I

The three novels in which Postal Inspector David Madden appears are all procedurals depicting the duties and methods of this oldest investigative branch of the United States government.[1] Disney not only follows Madden as he investigates a particular case but also refers in passing to other duties and other cases. Sometimes we get what might be described as "a day in the life of a postal inspector." Madden not only investigates such infractions as blackmail, poison pen letters, and use of the mails to defraud (one novel is built around each of these), but also has responsibility for a variety of other postal matters. A striking example occurs in *Black Mail*, when Madden learns of an airplane crash and, knowing that mail was aboard, rushes to the site. Disney develops this scene fully, and it is both moving in itself and illuminating for what it shows of Madden's work and his personality (coincidentally it is functional, for he discovers at the crash-site a letter which gives him an important clue) (see pp. 121-30).

In each of the three Madden novels, Disney acknowledged her indebtedness to members of the postal service, and she clearly tried hard to depict that service as accurately as possible. This goal created several difficulties which she overcame with varying degrees of success. First, she was limited to crimes in the jurisdiction of a postal inspector. Her preferred solution of this difficulty was to have a postal infraction lead to murder; Madden and the police then work together--Madden, of course, concentrating on postal matters but his investigation also leading to the solution of the murder. There was also the danger that Madden might become important only for what he does and not for what he is and thus lack human interest. This difficulty she tried to solve through careful characterization.

Madden is described as tall (5'11"),[2] He is dark and

"his thin face . . . had a thoughtful, scholarly expression touched with the reserve of one who withheld something of himself from others" (*Black Mail*, pp. 39-40). That expression is explained as "partly innate, partly acquired through years of withholding judgment in a job where no one must be taken quickly on trust."[3] His objectivity and understanding are frequently apparent in his behavior. For example, in *Black Mail*, he listens sympathetically to the protestations of a young woman who has received a defamatory letter:

> When people received poison pen letters they had to be allowed time to deny the accusations made, he assured and reassured that he didn't believe they were true. It would never do for him to say that the accusations were none of his business anyway; that, whether they were true or not, his business was to prevent the mails being used to send them. (p. 45)

Only a few details from Madden's private life are given us: he is a stamp collector, his boyhood interest in that hobby having perhaps led indirectly to his choice of profession (*Unappointed Rounds*, p. 58). More poignant is the fact that he is a lonely widower. His wife had been dearly loved, and at least once in each book something touches off memories of her and their life together. For instance, in *Black Mail*,

> The memory, the ghost of pain rather than pain itself, stirred in David Madden as he thought of his dead wife. It was part of the past now, the first shock and anguish of the doctor's words, the futile operation, the hospital room where he had watched his wife die a little day by day until, a shell of herself, she gave up the struggle and went away in her sleep while he sat beside her, her hand in his. He had thought himself prepared for her death. But when it came he had learned that there was no such thing as being prepared for the death of the person you loved best in the world. At first it had seemed like the end of everything, the pain and loss unbearable. He'd had no choice, though, except to live with it. (p. 57)

Though Madden is a lonely man who lives primarily through and for his work, he is not self-pitying and has not withdrawn from human concerns and relationships. His apartment is sterile and uncared for, but he often takes some attractive woman out to dinner. Indeed, an important thread in *Unappointed Rounds* is his attraction to the woman who is first a blackmail victim and then chief suspect in the murder of the blackmailer. He admonishes himself to keep his objectivity about her, but he is pleased to be able to prove her innocence, and at the end of the novel he is looking forward to asking her out to dinner. And in each of the other two novels he has a rather avuncular relationship with a young man whom, with both amusement and pleasure, he watches fall in love.

Madden, then, is likable. He inspires confidence in other characters, and the reader quickly comes to admire him. He is meticulous as an investigator and humane in dealing with victims and suspects. He is not, however, very well rounded as a character. While the devices of his stamp collecting, widowerhood, and dinner dates are helpful in establishing him as a person with a life outside of his working hours, they do not bring him alive. And no growth or change occurs in him.

II

Created for Disney's third novel, Jefferson DiMarco, claim adjuster for Commonwealth Insurance Company, was her most frequently used detective and continued longest in use (his last appearance was in 1971, although half of the novels in this series were published during the 1950s). Unlike Madden, he was not limited to any particular sort of crime, and unlike O'Neill, a county detective, he was not restricted in geographical location. He could go anywhere and investigate any murder in which the victim was one of his company's policy holders. The greater flexibility he offered doubtless explains Disney's wider use of him.

Disney is consistent in portraying him, but changes can be noted. Physical descriptions are unvarying in stressing his olive complexion, below-average height, and thick waistline. His reputation as a detective and his methods of working are also carried consistently from novel to novel. His relationship with his superior is one of mutual respect, though they carry on a half-serious war of words over Jeff's love of good living, his tendency to submit high (though honest) expense accounts, and his dislike of writing reports. He relies largely on "patient, tireless work"[4] to get results, but intuition sparked by an ability to empathize with others is as important to him as it is to Disney's other detectives.

Among details used to humanize and individualize Jeff, most prominent are his love of good food and the consequent concern over his weight (these appear in all eight of his novels though they tend to increase in frequency as we move chronologically through the books). His hobby is fishing, mentioned in several novels but particularly important in *Find the Woman*, which is set in a Maine resort area. Although he becomes involved in physical action more often than either Madden or O'Neill (always unhappily and not always successfully), he is also a man who likes to read, in several novels retreating to his hotel to read in bed. Perhaps most striking is a motif in *Find the Woman*: learning that each night some bears come to raid the garbage at a fishing camp, he repeatedly goes to watch them and finds them both awesome and touching.[5]

Two important sorts of changes can be noted in Disney's treatment of Jeff, though neither suggests carelessness on her part. The first is a growth in the fullness and depth of his characterization. She seems gradually to have come to know him better and thus to present him more complexly. The first two novels, *Dark Road* and *Family Skeleton*, offer little personal information about him, and that generally is in scattered phrases or modifiers. But by the fourth book, *Trick or Treat*, more personal information is given and it tends to appear in fully developed passages. In every case, however, the additional information is quite consistent with what we already knew, sometimes explaining or deepening our understanding of what had been told us earlier.[6]

The other change in Disney's treatment of Jeff is of more interest. Through the first six novels he is described as a bachelor with no ties; we learn that he has "Latin blood,"[7] lives in a "pleasant bachelor apartment,"[8] has risen from a childhood in a Boston tenement,[9] and despite a "sentimental streak" (*Dark Road*, p. 177) is unsympathetic with an acquaintance who uses an old rolltop desk because of its family associations (*Did She Fall or Was She Pushed?* p. 74). But in *Find the Woman* that apartment has rather surprisingly (to Jeff if not to the reader) given way to a home of his own.

> He had bought a house in Concord on one of the old streets near the center of the town. . . . It was a small, story-and-a-half house, built in 1771. He was now discovering in himself pride of ownership, a sense of putting down roots. . . . The most secret part of his feeling of pride came from the fact that he, the son of Italian immigrants, now owned a house that had been in existence in April 1775. It was possible that its then owner had been one of the embattled farmers who stood to face the British regulars at Concord Bridge. One of these days Jeff meant to find out, to trace the history of his house back to its beginnings. (pp. 22-3)

In this first year of his ownership he is fixing up the house, building a garage and beginning to take a hesitant interest in his yard. The last novel in the series, set nine years later, continues the process, for there we learn that his interest in gardening has grown, that "nowadays only the thought of looking ridiculous kept him out of garden shows, which, to his regret, seemed to be mostly a feminine province."[10]

Jeff, then, is a more complex character than David Madden. As a result he is more interesting, and this (along with the greater variety of the novels in which he is involved) perhaps helps explain his greater popularity.[11] In clearly and effectively portraying him, Disney showed her ability both to increase her own understanding of a potentially complex character and to make that character grow and develop.

III

Jim O'Neill, detective for Hampton County, Connecticut, was the first of Disney's three detectives to be created and the first to be discarded (the final book in which he appears was published in 1954, two years before Madden was invented and before five of the eight DiMarco books were written). Nevertheless, he is in many ways the most interesting of the three. He is the most fully developed, and he is the only one to undergo truly significant change and growth. In fact, each of the five books in his series develops a different stage in his life, from bachelorhood to the settled life of a *paterfamilias*. In the last three of his novels, Jim's family situation parallels in some way the situation or events of the mystery, and his wife is instrumental in leading him to discover the truth about the mystery.

When we first meet Jim in *A Compound for Death*, he is described as "a man in his late thirties with an easy, pleasant smile and an affable manner. . . . He was above medium height with an unremarkable set of features, a thick crown of black hair and brilliant hazel eyes. . . . He looked capable and intelligent, . . . a man who knew his business."[12] The details of his appearance, as we would expect, are kept consistent in the other novels, although Disney relies less on pure physical description in characterizing him than she does with Madden and DiMarco, perhaps for the very reason that she does so much more with his personal life. Of other details used in this novel, the most revealing relate to the boarding house in which he lives, maintaining cordial relations with his landlady despite his carelessness with cigarettes (p. 210, for example). Like both Madden and DiMarco, he relates well to people, and his methods of detection are very similar to theirs. He gives painstaking attention to detail and has moments of intuitive insight, although, we are told, he is "comfortably unaware" of the part played in his thought by psychological analysis (p. 104).

Like *A Compound for Death*, *Murder on a Tangent* is a true mystery, and in both we meet the characters involved in the mystery before we are introduced to Jim. The latter novel opens at a community service house (where murder will later occur), and we are quickly introduced to a number of the people who work there, including Margaret Lawrence, a 28-year-old social worker who has been employed there for three years.[13] When Jim and Margaret meet, they are quickly attracted to each other, though each must overcome stereotyped ideas of the other's profession. He is surprised to discover that a social worker can be attractive, not dowdy and plain (p. 73), and she is startled to find that he is not a tough, burly bully (p. 75). As they become better acquainted, Jim is even more surprised to realize that he is attracted to her intelligence:

> She was upsetting all his previous ideas about what he liked in women. She had intelligence, and he had hitherto shunned women with brains. She had none of the wiles and artifices that had hitherto amused him in women. Not a smitch of the clinging vine about her. She was swell. (p. 153)

Their relationship develops nicely as the book continues. We see them gradually come to know each other as they discuss their work and learn to tease each other (pp. 149-51, for instance). Their first kiss occurs naturally; no passionate scene, it demonstrates to Margaret that Jim will not be a romantic lover, but she decides that she really doesn't mind (p. 185). At the end of the novel nothing is settled between them. The last lines, however, are promising: "He smiled at her. 'You can stick around. I don't mind!'" (p. 209).[14]

In *Appointment at Nine*, the next O'Neill story, Margaret appears before Jim:

> When the telephone rang at eleven-thirty that night, Margaret O'Neill was awake to answer it. She was sitting in the dark in the living room enduring the heartburn that had lately become a daily part of her existence. As she walked out to the hall she belched and liquid fire rose in her throat. . . .
> There was a certain petty satisfaction in having a legitimate reason for awakening her husband. After all, it was his child, too, and there he lay, flat on his back, sleeping the sleep of those to whom the discomforts of pregnancy are unknown.[15]

Throughout this novel, their absorption in Margaret's pregnancy is a constant motif, Jim's preoccupation with his murder case being shown to be particularly deep by his occasional lapses of interest in Margaret's condition.

The qualities Jim values in Margaret are those he had become aware of earlier: her intelligence, straightforwardness, and sense of humor. He discusses the case with her, finding her psychological insights helpful (pp. 88-92), and her experience as a social worker gives her special knowledge regarding questionable circumstances regarding childbirth, a key aspect of this case (pp. 165-7). Her contributions to his solution are important, and her happy, though uncomfortable, pregnancy and the creation of their normal family both parallel and contrast with motifs in the mystery proper. In addition, Margaret's influence helps Jim learn to know himself better. As we have seen, Disney had dommented in *A Compound for Death* on the element of unexamined intuition in Jim's work. Margaret helps him recognize that element.

> Je decided to tell Margaret she was affecting his thought channels. There were never any two-dimensional conclusions, no straightforward cause and result. She had to go underneath all that. Perhaps he had always done that himself more than he realized, but Margaret was making him more aware of it. (p.152)

The O'Neill marriage, then, is clearly a happy one, and Disney several times stresses the difference it has made in Jim's life and feelings.

> He was always glad to go home to her after hours of separation. Time, that once had no meaning to him when he had a problem to solve, had become important. Days were compartmented into hours that he worked and evenings with his wife. And now that she was going to have a baby it was more important than ever that he get home. Alone in the house Margaret might have a fall, she might become ill, any number of dire things might happen. (p. 133)

And the last lines of the novel reemphasize this theme, leaving it as one of the more memorable aspects of the novel.

Fire at Will, the fourth of the O'Neill mysteries, opens with the motif of Jim's joy in his family, which now consists of Margaret and three-year-old Sarah. Margaret has become interested in community activities, being active in the Women's League.[16] The mystery involves neighbors of theirs; once again he consults with Margaret and finds her insights helpful. The family involved has a very tangled history, and the normality of the O'Neills' relationship runs in counterpoint to its destructiveness. But the O'Neills are not idealized. Small Sarah is mischievous and often a pest. She is unintentionally responsible for Jim's breaking his ankle (p. 52); immobilized, he must detect from his home, with Sarah serving as a frequent distraction--sometimes amusing and sometimes infuriating. Indeed, Sarah is a thoroughly realistic and utterly charming portrait of a small child. Characterization of Jim, both professionally and personally, is consistent with the earlier novels, for the changes are those of ordinary growth. His relationship with Margaret is as it had been in *Appointment at Nine*, and she is changed only as one might expect a young wife and mother to change as she becomes more a part of her community with roots and a growing family.

The Last Straw, the final novel in the O'Neill series,

takes Jim and his family a step further. Five years have passed, for Sarah is now eight, and Loria, four, has been added.[17] The O'Neills have acquired a house on a lake, where they spend the summers (pp. 27, 37). Their lakeside neighbors are involved in this mystery, so once again Jim's work impinges on his private life, and once again Margaret's understanding of personalities makes her able to contribute to his solution of the crime. Motifs from the last two books are repeated. The family scenes are warmly human and often comic. The children are as effectively depicted as Sarah was in *Fire at Will*. As before, they are not idealized: we see Sarah in a very typical tantrum (p. 115) and Loria causing a crisis by carelessly spilling grape juice on a guest (p. 101). The family pets are equally well depicted: Juney, an adult male cat, terrorizes Rex, a beagle puppy. Once again, Jim's happy marriage contrasts with a marriage which he must come to understand in order to solve the mystery. That marriage, of a weak young man and a selfish and grasping young woman, lacks all the qualities of companionship, humor, and understanding love which Jom and Margaret have built. And Margaret, who comprehends that other marriage first, gradually leads Jim to understand it and thus to solve the mystery.

The one significant inconsistency between this novel and the other O'Neill books is in the treatment of Margaret. Whereas earlier Disney had stressed Margaret's honesty and straightforwardness, her lack of feminine wiles, now she depicts Margaret as a conscious manipulator and Jim as aware of this and amused by it. Hints at the "tribulations" that had impeded Margaret's "triumphant arrival at the altar" (p. 38) hardly seem consistent with the courtship we saw beginning in *Murder on a Tangent*. And we are told of Margaret's view that

> A man should be the head of his own house, the way Jim was the head of his—or rather, she corrected herself with all honesty—the way Jim and the rest of the world thought he was. Whenever she did arrange things to go as she felt they should, she at least kept hidden the devices she employed. (p. 40)

That Jim actually is aware of her strategems is revealed a few pages later, when he contrasts her with another woman, who is very direct in getting what she wants: "She's right out in the open about it. Most of us beat around the bush. You, for instance. You're a great little bush beater" (p. 44). Perhaps it is significant that this novel, with its unexpected depiction of Margaret, once a straightforward, independent professional woman, now a manipulator of her man, was published in 1954, that time of complacency and of women's retreat from the marketplace into the home. Even those community activities so prominent in *Fire at Will* are absent here, another evidence of Margaret's participation in the retreat into domesticity of the 1950s which Betty Friedan was to document so tellingly in *The Feminine Mystique* less than a decade later.

But the characterization of Jim remains consistent. One may wonder why Disney now dropped him. The following year she returned to DiMarco (*Trick or Treat*), and another year later came the first of the Madden novels (*Unappointed Rounds*). Perhaps having carried Jim to a mature position as a family man she had little further interest in him. With

11

Madden she had the new worlds of the Post Office to explore, and with DiMarco she had the greater freedom offered by an insurance investigator who can go anywhere and investigate any murder in which an insurance holder might be victimized. The O'Neill mysteires are unlike the others in that a really significant part of our attention and emotional involvement is with the detective himself and the progress of his own life.[18] Perhaps she had developed him as far as she was interested and wished to turn to other characters and other situations.

IV

Disney tended to make less and less use of continuing cetectives as her career progressed. She published approximately 49 novels, between 1943 and 1976. By 1956, she had published twenty novels, of which eleven, over half, contained one of the continuing detectives. From 1957 on, 29 novels appeared, only six, or about one-fifth, contained one of her three detectives.[19] She began by working in well established forms, for the first two novels are true mysteries (as are four of the five O'Neill stories). She early experimented with the inverted mystery; the third novel (the first DiMarco story) falls into that category. And she soon began experimenting with yet other forms, though sometimes returning to the established ones. However, as time went on, she less often restricted herself to a particular form, many of the later novels seeming to take their impetus from a particular character or relationship or situation. The later novels are not necessarily better than the earlier ones, though the level of craftsmanship is remarkably even. What these later novels show is an ever increasing freedom to experiment, to write the kind of novel that a particular character or situation logically calls for, whatever be the label that might be attached to it.

In summing up Disney's uses of her three continuing detectives, one might observe that she began with Jim O'Neill, first drew him with broad strokes and then developed him more fully and carried him through logical, typical stages of life. She got to know him better, and she made him grow and change in a believable way. Jeff DiMarco, the second to be created, was also sketch ed briefly in his first several novels. He changed little in his first six novels, but Disney grew to know him better and so his characterization became fuller. In his last two novels, he underwent change, believably depicted but nowhere nearly so great as that of Jim O'Neill. Dave Madden, last to be created, was fully portrayed from the beginning, but he never changed. Perhaps in first drawing him in 1956, after all of the O'Neill and half of the DiMarco books had been written, she profited by the experiences of writing the earlier books.

In any event, Disney's achievement with these men is no small one. She managed to make all of them believable human beings. All are professionals and good at their jobs, but all have a certain detachment and the ability to laugh at themselves. Not particularly outstanding in any way, neither tough nor eccentric, they are men we might like to meet--but not to have as adversaries.

NOTES

[1] *Black Mail* (Garden City, NY: Doubleday & Company, Inc., 1958), p. 40. After first footnotes to all Disney novels, citations will be made parenthetically in the text.

[2] *Unappointed Rounds* (Garden City, NY: Doubleday & Company, Inc., 1956), p. 12.

[3] *Mrs. Meeker's Money* (Garden City, NY: Doubleday & Company, Inc., 1961), p. 32.

[4] *Straw Man* (Garden City, NY: Doubleday & Company, Inc., 1951), p. 154.

[5] (Garden City, NY: Doubleday & Company, Inc., 1962), p. 54.

[6] It is worth noting that *Trick or Treat* appeared in 1955, after all five O'Neill books had been published (see below); it was in fact her nineteenth novel, so we are observing here a sign of her increasing skill as a novelist.

[7] *Dark Road* (Garden City, NY: Doubleday & Company, Inc., 1946), p. 177.

[8] *Family Skeleton* (New York: Berkley Publishing Corp., 1972), p. 101.

[9] *Did She Fall or Was She Pushed?* (Garden City, NY: Doubleday & Company, Inc., 1959), p. 21.

[10] *The Chandler Policy* (New York: G.P. Putnam's Sons, 1971), p. 36.

[11] His novels have been more frequently reprinted than Madden's. Steinbrunner and Penzler mention both Madden and DiMarco, but give a separate entry only to DiMarco. O'Neill, oddly enough, is not mentioned at all. (See *Encyclopedia of Mystery and Detection*, NY: McGraw-Hill, 1976).

[12] (New York: Walter J. Black, Inc., 1943), p. 20.

[13] (Garden City, NY: Doubleday, Doran and Co., Inc., 1945), pp. 22, 24.

[14] An experienced reader, however, would not necessarily expect to meet Margaret in later works. The end of *Unappointed Rounds* was similar, but the woman in question there is not mentioned in the succeeding Madden novels.

[15] (Garden City, NY: Doubleday & Company, Inc., 1947), p. 24.

[16] (New York: Manor Books, Inc., 1976), pp. 44, 117, 165-70.

[17] (New York: Popular Library, 1954), p. 27.

[18] Perhaps a parallel may be drawn with the last two of Dorothy L. Sayers' Wimsey novels. *Gaudy Night* and *Busman's Honeymoon* have often been considered less effective *as mysteries* than the earlier books, because so much attention is given to Lord Peter's and Harriet's relationship, and this, it is said, detracts from the mysteries. I would maintain that the last two Wimsey books, but especially *Gaudy Night*, are best *as novels* because the characterization is more complex and the thematic concerns dramatized in the Peter-Harriet relationship and in the mysteries are more significant and more maturely handled. In a lesser way, the same

case may be made for the O'Neill mysteries among Disney's corpus.

[19] Taking another cut-off point, we find that in the last thirteen years of her career, 1963-1976, only one Disney novel out of the eighteen published dealt with one of the continuing detectives.

(continued from p. 49) in *The Pro-Am Murders* though Welch has assumed the pseudonym Patrick Cake. Still, we have the quintessential Quince: masochistic, sexy (every page, Dion?), and violent. Employing an unusual twist, the author has included many blurry pictures of a golf tournament. As a mystery it does not offer much, and the pictures do little to advance the plot. It proves that one good word is worth 53 pictures. Still, it may be of some interest to golf fans because of its background: the annual Bing Crosby Pro-Amateur Golf Tournament in Pebble Beach, California. It is available for $8.95 through The Proteus Press 250 Thunderbird Drive Aptos, California 95003.

THE INVESTIGATION
FICTION AND FACT
By Jo Ann Vicarel

In July, 1965, five year old Eddie and four year old Missy Crimmins disappeared from their bedroom in Queens. Within a week their bodies had been found. The intensive investigation that followed culminated three years later in the conviction of their mother Alice for the manslaughter of Missy. The conviction was appealed and reversed in Appelate Court. Mrs. Crimmins was brought to trial a second time in 1971, when she was tried not only for the manslaughter of Missy, but the murder of Eddie. She was convicted of murder in the first degree and sentenced to life imprisonment. In 1973 the Appellate Division reversed the murder conviction; and the reversal was upheld in 1975 but the manslaughter conviction was upheld and Alice Crimmins was returned to prison to complete her sentence.

Dorothy Uhnak's *The Investigation* (NY: Simon and Schuster, 1977) is a well written, "edge of the chair" police story based on the real story of Alice Crimmins. *The Investigation* follows the lines of the Crimmins case closely, but Dorothy Uhnak knows when to bend the facts to write good fiction. She uses the actual events to her best advantage and produces a first rate novel deserving of its bestseller status.

Two little boys, Georgie and Terry Keeler disappear from their bedroom in an apartment complex in Queens. Because of a police staff shortage, the Queens District Attorney's Investigation Squad catches the case and remains in charge even after the boys' bodies are found, making the case a double homicide.

Complications set in as the detectives go to work. Kitty and George Keeler are separated; the mother is beautiful and leads a swinging life full of manfriends, among which are a high placed New York politician and several organized crime and underworld figures. The police seize upon Kitty as the most likely suspect. She was alone with the children; she was nursing Georgie who had measles, with Terry a certainty to have them next; and she had to cancel a business cum pleasure trip to Phoenix because of the sickness. Looking at her apartment and her clothing, the police figure Kitty to be inclined to think of herself first. They reason she could have killed the children in a rage of frustration. She becomes the sole focus of the investigation: after all, who else could have done it and for what reason?

The story is told by Detective Joe Peters who is active in the police investigation. He is the first to speak with Kitty and George at the scene of the disappearance and escorts George to the vacant lot where the bodies are found. Peters is party to the subsequent interviews and interrogations of witnesses and privy to the closed door conferences with the DA. He knows that the police are not conducting an unbiased inquiry, so he launches an independent investigation of his own to arrive at the truth. And he does.

Dorothy Uhnak has taken the Alice Crimmins story and has sorted and arranged those events into a most satisfying tale with a neat, plausible solution. But the real case is not that easy to understand.

For anyone interested in crime and murder cases and/or the Crimmins case, two books have been written about it. George Carpozi, Jr. wrote *Ordeal by Trial: The Alice Crimmins Case* (N.Y.: Walker and Company, 1972) and the other work is Kenneth Gross' *The Alice Crimmins Case* (N.Y.: Alfred A. Knopf, 1975).

Carpozi and Gross are veteran New York newspaper reporters who write books about crime.* Carposi covered the Crimmins story for the now defunct *NY Journal-American*. He concentrates on the trials and the wheels of criminal justice. He says he had tried to write an unbiased account of the Crimmins affair and he has done that to a degree. Most of his book is a reqorking of the newspaper accounts with one or two new tidmits.

Probably the more interesting book, for me at least, is Kenneth Gross' account, as he had access to information which did not come out at either trial and he interviewed people who were not called to give evidence, plus he attempts to refute several points made by key witnesses for the prosecution. He presents the police investigation and the District Attorney's procedures as nothing less than biased. Certainly, the extensive use of wiretaps, harrassing of witnesses, entrapment tactics, invasion of privacy, and the openly biased court rulings of the first trial point to a one sided investigation and prosecution. Alice Cummins was the only suspect. The police never took her husband Edmund seriously, yet the Crimmins were engaged in a custody fight and points of Crimmins story did not check out.

Gross also mentions the "pants" burglar who was operating in Queens at the time of the Crimmins case and who had attempted to take a child from an apartment. The burglar only broke into occupied apartments and robbed the money from the man's pants pocket. His/her operations ceased when the children were murdered.

Carpozi and Gross have written good books, informative and thought provoking. Both writers believe that justice was not done, that the whole truth was not told, and that we still do not know what happened that night in July, 1965, when two innocent children were murdered and their mother was catipulted into one of the most puzzling investigations of the century.

*George Carpozi has written *The Chicago Nurse Murders* and Kenneth Gross co-authored *Victims* about the Janice Wylie-Emily Hoffert murders in New York which was later made into the pilot movie for the *Kojak* TV series. Incidentally, Kenneth Gross interview Alice Crimmins for *Newsday* and, to my knowledge, it is the only interview she has ever granted. Some of her personal reminiscences are included in his book.

To add to the credentials of the three authors discussed, Dorothy Uhnak was a member of the New York Transit Police for several years and wrote a book about her experiences entitled *Policewoman*. She brings alot of authenticity to any police procedural she writes.

IT'S ABOUT CRIME
Notes on Recent Reading
By Marvin Lachman

The first question that occurs regarding Allen J. Hubin's *The Bibliography of Crime Fiction 1749-1975* is whether it is worth the high price, $59.95, being asked by Publisher's Inc. Drawer P, Del Mar, California 92014. If you've bought a copy, you've already made a preliminary decision. For those aware of this book and considering purchase of either a personal copy or for a library, I hope to provide some guidance.

The casual mystery fan will probably not need (or want) this book. I say this with no intent to deprecate that person whose interest in our addiction extends only to the point of enjoying a good story. Without this type of reader, who over the years has consumed millions of copies of Doyle, Rinehart, Gardner, and Christie, it would not have been economically feasible for our field to have blossomed.

Those of you who are reading this column probably fit into another category. Your interest is such that you will enjoy tremendously such features of this book as:

1. An alphabetical list of every author who had published a mystery novel, volume of short stories, or play. This includes pseudonyms, and in many cases the years of birth and death.

2. An alphabetical listing of each author's books, with first British and American publishers and years of publication. Titles which changed in crossing the Atlantic are usefully identified.

3. Information as to which books are about series characters. There is also a very helpful alphabetical index of these series characters.

4. A tremendous improvement in both accuracy and completeness over Ordean Hagen's *Who Done It* (1969), the pioneer work which this book has updated. Hubin gives due credit to Hagen but modestly leaves to the reader's imagination most of the tremendous effort his own book involved.

On the negative side, one must note the following:

1. The price. I grant that it is difficult to put a value on this to the true fanatic, but $60 is expensive for a work without illustrations and with small print. A 230 page title index consumes 33% of the book's space and seems, in cost/benefit terms, not worth it. It is useful if you are thinking of a title and cannot recall the author, but this would not seem to be a pressing need. It would have been preferable to have been able to cut the price by one third. The title index also provides some "fun" information for trivia nuts--e.g. there have been eight mysteries entitled *Nightmare*. Be prepared for some future articles by yours truly, in my "Mysterious Miscellaneous Mish-Mash" series, about mystery titles.

2. The book was out of date when it was published. However, that is inevitable with reference books, and a supplement every five years is promised. Let us hope the cost will not be prohibitive. Meanwhile, there is generous marginal space to permit do-it-yourselfers to annotate and update their copies.

Librarians must be aware that many of their "customers"

come for the mystery fiction. This bibliography can lure them into the reference section by providing answers to many of their questions, including the titles of other works by mystery authors they enjoy.

Eight plays by Agatha Christie have been collected by Dodd-Mead in *The Mousetrap and Other Plays* ($12.95). Three are well known "blockbusters," like the titular work, *Ten Little Indians* and *Witness for the Prosecution*. There are also the lesser known *Appointment with Death*, *The Hollow*, *Towards Zero*, *Go Back for Murder* and *Verdict*, with some surprises for those readers familiar with the original novels on which the first four are based.

Ira Levin, best-selling novelist and playwright provides an excellent introduction in which he aptly characterizes the kind of play she writes as "...theater that grips and dazzles and surprises." He might also have quoted Ira Levin who, in his comedy *Critic's Choice*, has a character comment, with sarcasm, on the almost infinite variety of Christie: "Once you've read fifty Agatha Christie's, you've read them all."

The fact that he handed me my "Edgar" in 1977 does not account for my feeling that Hillary Waugh is a fine mystery writer. Books like *Last Seen Wearing* (1952), *A Rag and a Bone* (1954), and *Prisoner's Plea* (1963) speak for themselves. Though Waugh's recent output has not been as impressive, he is still active, and there is much pleasure to be obtained from digging out older Waugh works. I recently read *Born Victim* (1962), another in Waugh's own sub-genre, the mystery about the missing teen-ager. What makes this b-ok so special is that the values of a good novel are combined with those of a good mystery. We care about the characters as we do in the best of Ross Macdonald or Margaret Millar. Only a somewhat disappointing ending, with questionable character motivation, prevents this from being a classic.

By coincidence, shortly after reading Waugh's book, I read a short story by Ruth Rendell in EQMM Sept. 1978 with the title "Born Victim." This is an adult story with a clever twist at the end but with some of the weakest motivation of all time.

To paraphrase Mark Twain, everyone talks about short stories, but no one does anything about them. At any rate, no one reviews them unless they are collected. Because I am delinquent in my reading, I can say very little about stories published thus far in 1979. However, there are some 1978 items in EQMM which should not go unnoticed.

I don't know who Ernest Savage is. I'm not aware of any novels he has written. Based on two EQMM stories "Count Me Out" (June 1978) and "Finders Weepers" (Sept. 1978) he is a potential great in that woefully neglected field: the hard-boiled short story. Speaking of super stars of the short story firmament, one thinks of Cornell Woolrich whose "Death Between Dances" (1947) was reprinted, I am glad to say, in EQMM for October 1978. It contains such archetypal Woolrichiana as: "She didn't scream. Death was too new to her. She barely knew what it was. She hadn't lived long enough." Watch the pages of this journal for "The Music of Cornell Woolrich" on which (along with about a dozen other pieces) I am currently working.

Edward D. Hoch writes more different types of short stories than any other writer past, present, *(continued on p. 49)*

THE BOOKS OF GEOFFREY HOMES

By Theodore P. Dukeshire

Born in California in 1902, Daniel Mainwaring learned about his native state at an early age by taking long wagon trips with his father who was a state forest ranger.

After graduating from Fresno State College, Mainwaring tried teaching for a year before starting a newspaper career with the *San Francisco Chronicle*.

It was during this period that Mainwaring, using the pseudonym Geoffrey Homes, began writing, using four main themes which are repeated throughout his books. They are: 1) Murder or another crime from the past which suddenly resurfaces. 2) Missing persons. Usually an heir or heiress. 3) The intertwined and tangled relationships usually found among families of the very rich. 4) Home's use of the California and Western backgrounds. His descriptions of the small coastal towns and other rural areas of the San Joaquin Valley show a deep love of his native state and surrounding areas of the West.

Homes's first detective hero, Robin Bishop, has a past which is sketchy at best. Once a reporter on a variety of newspapers, Bishop, for unknown reasons, became a nomad and rode the rails from town to town seeking work at various dude ranches and lumber camps. Bishop was on a three week drunk when Oscar Morgan found him and gave him a job as legman (later he became a partner) with Morgan & Co. which led to Robin's first recorded case, *The Man Who Murdered Himself*.

When the body of Robert Hastings is found in the city reservoir, oscar Morgan and Robin try to get a share of the insurance money by attempting to locate Hastings's relatives. A gangster's missing daughter, complicated family relationships, murder from the past, and finally murder in the present complicate matters, but Robin finally solves the case and manages to gain a wife and find himself.

> . . . It occurred to him [Robin] suddenly that he wasn't interested in the money they would make from the case. He cared not a rap for that. It was as though he was a reporter again on the track of a story. He wanted to find out what happened—that was all . . .

A reporter in *The Doctor Died at Dusk*, Bishop finds himself in Morgantown covering a strike by the fruit pickers when, during a street riot, shooting breaks out and Dr. Seymour Morgan is found shot in his office. When neither Morgan's father nor his wife grieve over his death, Bishop decides to find out why. Again tangled family relationships play a major part in solving the case.

Murder from the past and intertwined relationships among friends form the basis of *The Man Who Didn't Exist*.

Robin and his wife, Mary, are out on the town in Point Utopia when Robin finds a man's coat lying on the beach and footprints heading toward the ocean. A suicide note signed Zenophan Zwick along with a newspaper clipping asking "Who is Zenophan Zwick?" are found in one of the pockets. Zwick, the world's most widely read mystery writer, has disappeared, and the five people who fit the clipping writer's qualifications all live in the same apartment house. . . .

Los Pinos, which Homes describes as, "Half buried in pine trees with the hills behind, the sea in front, and the valley to the left was a pretty town," is the setting for *The Man Who Murdered Goliath*.

Goliath is Walter K. Miller, a ruthless millionaire, who made many enemies on his climb to the top.

Calling the *Los Pinos Herald*, Miller says he's tired of life and is going to kill himself, a shot is heard over the phone, and Miller is found dead in his living room. Robin Bishop, investigating Miller's death, finds tangled family relationships, a suicide some years earlier that Miller supposedly copied, and traces of Miller's past which lead straight to Los Pinos.

Homes's second detective hero, Humphrey Campbell, has a past that is as vague as Robin Bishop's. Campbell once ran liquor into Key West and had some trouble with the booze. Now the only thing he drinks is milk. Described as "fat", Humphrey says, "It's not fat, it's muscle." In his first recorded case, *Then There Were Three*, Humphrey traces heiress Marjorie Keenan to Los Pinos where he meets Robin Bishop. When Marjorie's body is found in a pet cemetary, both Humphrey and Robin work together to solve the case.

The search for a millionaire's missing son takes Humphrey to Reno, Nevada, and the middle of a bank robbery. When one of the robbers thinks he's seen Humphrey before, Humphrey realizes the case of *No Hands on the Clock* may be more complex than he thought. Framed for murder, a gay divorcee who has her sights square on Humphrey, along with a shoot-out in the Nevada desert prove Humphrey right.

When Michael Burke hires Humphrey to find out if he's the heir to the large Dunecht estate, murder follows in *Finders Keepers*. An old diary which seems to prove Burke's claim also brings to light a thirty year old murder in the Dunecht family.

The ax murder of Irene Peck, the ex-mother-in law of Joseph Borden, is Humphrey's next case in *Forty Whacks*. Borden, an ex-concert pianist, had his right hand chopped off by Irene Peck during an family argument. Now living on a barge, Humphrey enters the case when his secretary believes Borden innocent of the murder.

In Humphrey Campbell's last case, *Six Silver Handles*, temporary amnesia plays a large part.

Serviceman Johnny Foster is hitchhiking when he's picked up by millionaire Warren Hastings. Hastings invites Johnny out to his house for a drink and Johnny accepts. Passing out after too much to drink, Foster wakes up to find Hastings murdered and the police pounding on the front door. Unfortunately, Johnny can't remember a thing. Since Humphrey only has a week before entering the service, he takes the case with misgivings. Fighting both a deadline, and his client who escaped jail and is suspected of a second murder, Humphrey has all he can do to solve the case and bring a multiple killer to justice.

Not as well known as Bishop and Campbell is Homes's third detective, Mexican Jose Manuel Madero. Described as dapper, Madero also feels terrible when he sees a woman in the Mexican hills carrying a load on her back. He also knits when he's thinking. Keeping very much in the background, Madero helps Mitchell Drake solve the murder of Drake's missing brother in *The Street of the Crying Woman*.

When he goes to Tucson, Arizona, Ben Logan gets Madero's help after he runs afoul of Nazis, murder and a budding revolution in *The Hill of the Terrified Monk*.

Murder from the past catches up with Red Bailey in Homes's only non-series book, *Build My Gallows High*.

Once Partners with Johnny Fisher in a detective agency, Bailey's on the run for Fisher's murder and is operating a small gas station in a Nevada town when their ex-client, Whit Sterling, finds him.

Originally hired by Sterling to find his girl friend, Mumsie McGonigle, and fifty thousand dollars she ran away with after shooting Sterling. Bailey finds her in Mexico and falls in love with her, only Fisher catches up with Bailey and Mumsie. . . .

Rehired by Sterling to steal some books from accountant, Leonard Eels, Bailey finds Eels's body and realizes that Sterling has put him on the spot. This time Bailey runs away again, trying to find a way to clear himself of a murder he didn't commit.

Homes was given the job of writing the movie script for *Gallows* which was retitled, *Out of the Past* for the screen. Other movie credits to Homes's/Mainwaring's credit include: The original *Invasion of the Body Snatchers*, *The Lawless*, *The Phoenix City Story* and *Baby Face Nelson*.

A GEOFFREY HOMES CHECKLIST

1. *Build My Gallows High*
   William Morrow, 1946; Ace Books, 1956
2. *The Doctor Died at Dusk*
   William Morrow, 1936
3. *Finders Keepers*
   William Morrow, 1940
4. *Forty Whacks*
   William Morrow, 1941
   PPk. Title: *Stiffs Don't Vote*, Bantam, 1947
5. *Hill of the Terrified Monk*
   William Morrow, 1943
   Ppk Title: *Dead as a Dummy*
6. *The Man Who Didn't Exist*
   William Morrow, 1937
7. *The Man Who Murdered Goliath*
   William Morrow, 1938
8. *The Man Who Murdered Himself*
   William Morrow, 1936
9. *No Hands on the Clock*
   William Morrow, 1939
10. *Six Silver Handles*
    William Morrow, 1944
    PPk Title: *The Case of the Unhappy Angels*
11. *The Street of the Crying Woman*
    William Morrow, 1942
    PPk Title: *The Case of the Mexican Knife*
    English Title: *Seven Died*
12. *Then There Were Three*
    William Morrow, 1938

THE NERO WOLFE SAGA
Part XIII
By Guy M. Townsend

"Poison à la Carte" [April 1958], published in *Three at Wolfe's Door*, 1960.
   THE STORY ::: "Lewis Hewitt, the millionaire and orchid fancier for whom Nero Wolfe had once handled a tough problem," talks Wolfe into loaning Fritz for one evening to the "Ten for Aristology", which, Hewitt explains, "was a group of ten men pursuing the idea of perfection in food and drink." The Ten want Fritz to cook their annual dinner for them, and after considerable hesitation Wolfe gives in and Fritz agrees to undertake the job. At the dinner, at which Archie and Wolfe are guests, one of the Ten becomes ill and dies (of arsenic poisoning), and Wolfe undertakes, successfully of course, to discover which of the twelve beautiful serving girls was so gauche as to use Fritz's splendid food as a vehicle for murder. Usually, Wolfe knows the identity of the guilty party and sets his traps to secure evidence. In this instance, however, he has no idea beforehand which of the women is guilty, but he turns her out by what Archie calls "one of the most elaborate charades Wolfe had ever staged."
   WOLFE ::: "Wolfe dislikes eating with strangers and thinks that more than six at table spoils a meal." Wolfe's weight remains at one seventh of a ton. Archie says that Wolfe succeeds in convincing Hewitt that "dining was not a science but an art." At one point Wolfe astounds Archie by telling him to go collect the serving girls, even though they were still eating their own meals--"It was hard to believe. They were eating; and for him to interrupt a man, or even a woman, at a meal, was unheard of. Not even me. Only in an extreme emergency had he ever asked me to quit food before I was through. Boiling was no name for it." Wolfe is so upset that when one of the men guests makes a remark, Wolfe dismisses it discourteously: "Nonsense. I am too provoked for civility." He also remarks, "I am not a tyro at inquiry." This next item could also go in the ROUTINE AT THE BROWNSTONE section:

> The daily schedule was messed beyond repair. When we had finally got home, at five o'clock in the morning, Wolfe had told Fritz to forget about breakfast until further notice, and had sent me up to the plant rooms to leave a note for Theodore saying that he would not appear at nine in the morning and perhaps not at all. It had been not at all. At half past eleven he had buzzed on the house phone to tell Fritz to bring up the breakfast tray with four eggs and ten slices of bacon instead of two and five, and it was past one o'clock when the sounds came of his elevator and then his footsteps in the hall, heading for the office.
>   If you think a problem child is tough, try handling a problem elephant. He is plenty knotty even when he is himself, and that day he was really special.

At one point Wolfe says, "My facilities, including my memory, are not impaired. I am merely ruffled beyond the bounds of tolerance", and Archie remarks that "for him that was an abject apology, and a sign that he was beginning to regain control." Archie says, "I returned to the office and found Wolfe sitting with his eyes closed and his fists planted on the chair arms"; he and Wolfe converse, so this isn't the same as the eyes-closed-lips-in-and-out routine. Wolfe does some fancy talking in this one: "A woman whose conscience has no sting will stop at nothing."

ARCHIE ::: Wolfe and Fritz appear to have similar opinions of Archie's way with the women. "Fritz likes to pretend that he has reason to believe that no damsel is safe within a mile of me, which doesn't make sense since you can't tell much about them a mile off, and I thought it would do him good to see me operate at close quarters", but he's somwhat embarrassed when Wolfe voices his opinion of Archie's prowess in front of others: "When we're alone I don't particularly mind his insinuations that I presume to be an authority on women, but there was company present." Archie observes in this one that "girls always look better in uniforms or costumes." He takes one of his irregular smokes this time out-- "I lit a cigar just to be doing something." And he drinks milk--"I can always drink milk and had preferred it to Bubble-Pagne, registered trademark, a dime a bottle, which they [several women] were having." Archie gets hauled in, by Purley, for obstructing justice.

OTHER REGULARS ::: Although Fritz does not have a great deal to say in this one, he is central to it and we do learn a bit more about him. First, Fritz is well-paid: "It took a big slice of his [Wolfe's] income as a private detective to pay Fritz Brenner, chef and housekeeper in the old brownstone on West 35th Street--about the same as the slice that came to me as his assistant detective and man Friday." Wolfe calls Fritz "one of my most valued friends." And Fritz is a pretty headstrong fellow. He refuses, for example, to commit himself to cooking for the Ten until he has personally inspected the kitchen in which he will have to work. Also, Archie says "ther is no one more obliging than Fritz, but also there is no one more immovable when he has taken a stand", even when that stand is against Wolfe himself. Finally, after Fritz learns that his cooking has been used to commit murder, Archie remarks, "I had once told Fritz that I could imagine no circumstances in which he would look really unhappy, but now I wouldn't have to try." And, oh yes, Archie tells Purley that Fritz is Wolfe's client in this case. As for Purley Stebbins, he is fairly hostile in this one: "He's a proud man, Purley is, and I wouldn't go so far as to say that he has nothing to be proud of. He's not a bad cop, as cops go." But Purley's disliking for Wolfe is unabated: "Purley nodded. He hates to answer questions from Wolfe." Archie also remarks, "He always gets hoarser as the tension grows; that's the only sign." Cramer makes a brief appearance, and Lt. Rowcliff is mentioned twice, though he does not a-pear; Archie tells Purley, "Even under arrest, one will get you five that I can make him [Rowcliff] start stuttering in ten minutes", and later Archie tells us that "it had taken me eight minutes to get him stuttering." Felix, from Rusterman's, plays a role in this one, as he and another Rusterman employee, Zoltan Mahany, help Fritz prepare the meal. "In a way Wolfe was Felix's boss. When Wolfe's oldest and dearest friend, Marko

Vukcic, who had owned Rusterman's restaurant, had died, his will had left the restaurant to members of the staff in trust, with Wolfe as the trustee, and Felix was the maître d'hôtel. "With that job at the best restaurant in New York, naturally Felix was both bland and commanding, but now he was neither." Wolfe says to him, "I have always found you worthy of trust, but it's possible that in your exalted position, maître d'hôtel at Rusterman's, you would rather dodge than get involved in a poisoning. Are you dodging, Felix?" Felix is not. Lastly, Nathaniel Parker is just mentioned.

ROUTINE AT THE BROWNSTONE ::: Re the doorbell: "The doorbell rang and I got up and went to the hall. At the rear the door to the kitchen swung open part way and Felix poked his head through, saw me, and withdrew"; when the doorbell rings at 2:25 in the afternoon, Fritz answers it.

"Method Three for Murder" [September 1958], published in *Three at Wolfe's Door*, 1960.

THE STORY ::: When Mira Holt finds a corpse in the back of the cab she has borrowed for the evening she drives to West Thirty-fifth Street in hopes of learning, without exposing her actual situation, how to dispose of the unwanted body. Her arrival at the brownstone coincides with Archie's departure from it--he and Wolfe have had a falling out and he has quit. Mira hires Archie, and a cop car pulls up as they are seated on the front stoop discussing the problem. Both pretend ignorance about the cab and its contents, and Wolfe invites them inside when he discovers the commotion made by the cops, who arrive on the scene en masse. He and Archie call a temporary truce and he accepts half of Archie's "retainer" to act with him in clearing Mira, who is soon taken away by Cramer. There is an adequate cast of suspects in this short tale, and the story is entertaining enough, though its strength derives more from the interest engendered by Archie's threatened resignation. Wolfe exposes the killer by logic, but without furnishing much in the way of proof.

WOLFE ::: "Since he weighs a seventh of a tone he always looks big, but when he's being obnoxious he looks even bigger." Wolfe is reading John Gunther's *Inside Russia Today*. This item takes place at shortly after 11 a.m.: "Wolfe, behind his desk, had been pouring beer when we entered." At one point Cramer sarcastically asks Wolfe, "Did you ever skip a meal in your life?" to which Wolfe replies, "Many times when I was younger, by necessity." Wolfe speaks of "our poor substitute for a neuter pronoun" in reference to having to say "he" when speaking of a person whose sex is not revealed. "Wolfe leaned back and shut his eyes, and his lips began to work. Irving started to say something, and I snapped at him, 'Hold it.' Wolfe pushed his lips out and pulled them in, out and in, out and in. . . . When he starts that lip operation the sparks are flying inside his skull." The odd thing here is that Archie bothers to shush Irving, since he has earlier said that when Wolfe is doing the lip routine nothing will disturb him.

ARCHIE ::: A woman mentions that the has seen Archie at the Flamingo. Archie mentions the seventh grade in Ohio. "It had been years since he had first told me that when I described a man he must see him and hear him, and I had learned the trick long ago. I also knew how to report conversations word for word."

WOLFE & ARCHIE ::: Archie's "resignation" is interesting in its own right and deserves additional attention for the light it sheds on his relations with Wolfe. Perhaps, therefore, extensive quotations will be forgiven.

> During the years I have worked for Nero Wolfe and lived under his roof, I have quit and been fired about the same number of times, say thirty or forty. Mostly we have been merely letting off steam, but sometimes we have meant it, more or less, and that Monday evening in September I was really fed up.

Archie was not fond of the main dish they had at dinner that day, and when, over after-dinner coffee in the office, he had mentioned having tentatively made an appointment for a friend with Wolfe for eleven the next morning without first clearing it, Wolfe told him to cancel it, and then proceeded to open his book. "If I had been a camel and the book had been a straw you could have heard my spine crack. He knew darned well he shouldn't have opened it until we had finished with coffee." Archie tries to explain; "He was holding the book open and his eyes were on it, but he spoke. 'You know quite well, Archie, that I must be consulted on appointments. . . . Phone him not to come. Tell him I have other engagements.'"

> So I quit. I admit that on some other occasions my quitting had been merely a threat, to jolt him into seeing reason, but not that time. When a mule plants its feet a certain way there's no use trying to budge it. I swiveled, got my memo pad, wrote on it, yanked the sheet off, got up and crossed to his desk, and handed him the sheet.
> "That's Anderson's number," I told him. "If you're too busy to phone him not to come, Fritz can. I'm through. I'll stay with friends tonight and come tomorrow for my stuff."
> His eyes had left the book to glare at me. "Pfui," he said.
> "I agree," I said. "Absolutely." I turned and marched out. I do not say that as I got my hat from the rack in the hall my course was clearly mapped for the next twenty years, or even twenty hours. Wolfe owned the house but not everything in it, for the furniture in my room on the third floor had been bought and paid for by me. That would have to wait until I found a place to move it to, but I would get my clothes and other items tomorrow.

Of course, Archie only gets as far as the stoop, and eventually Wolfe actually comes to the front door and demands to know "What's going on?" When Archie explains, Wolfe says.

> "Why didn't you bring Miss Holt inside?"
> "Because it's not my house. Or my office."
> "Nonsense. There is the front room. If you wish to stand on ceremony, I invite you to use it for consultation with your client."

After they get inside, and Archie explains certain things to Wolfe which he couldn't do outside with Cramer listening in, Archie says he and Mira will just use the back door to make their getaway before Cramer comes in and gets them.

"NO." Wolfe snapped it. "This is preposterous. Give me half of that fifty dollars."

I raised a brow. "For what?"

"To pay me. You have helped me with many problems; surely I can help you with one. I am not being quixotic. I do not accept your headstrong decision that our long association has ended, but even if it has, your repute is inextricably involved with mine. Your client is in a pickle. I have never tried to do a job without your help; why should you try to do one without mine?"

I wanted to grin at him, but he might have misunderstood.

"Okay," I said, and got a twenty from the pocket where I had put the fee, and a five from my wallet, and handed them to him.

Archie soon learns that Wolfe is observing some slightly different rules, since this is Archie's client. For example, Cramer decides to take Mira in for questioning--

I was sitting with my jaw set. Wolfe would rather miss a meal than let Cramer or any other cop take a client of his from that office into custody, and over the years I have seen and heard him pull some fancy maneuvers to prevent it. But this was my client, and he wasn't batting an eye. I admit that it would have had to be something extra fancy, and it was up to me, not him, but I had split the fee with him.

Also, Archie does a good bit of questioning in this one, while Wolfe sits by and listens with his eyes closed. Finally, here is how the tiff is resolved: Archie suggests setting up an appointment for eleven the next morning.

"Make it a quarter past eleven," he said. "I will be engaged until then with Mr. Anderson."

I opened my mouth and closed it again. "Didn't you phone him not to come?"

"On the contrary, I phoned him to come. On reflection I saw that I had been hasty. In my employ, as my agent, you had made a commitment, and I was bound by it. I should not have repudiated it. I should have honored it, and then dismissed you if I considered your disregard of the rules intolerable."

"I see. I can understand that you'd rather fire me than have me quit."

"I said 'if.'"

OTHER REGULARS ::: Lon Cohen gets called a few times and supplies some information, and in the end Archie calls him the instant the exposure of the killer takes place to make good his promise to give him the scoop. Archie thinks about calling Nathaniel Parker, but doesn't do it. Purley Stebbins makes an appearance--Archie mentions "his broad, burly shoulders"--as does Cramer, who grabs a woman's arm to keep her from talking to someone and gets slapped for his pains. Fritz is present in the background.

ROUTINE AT THE BROWNSTONE ::: "I had disregarded another rule by bringing in a visitor without consulting Wolfe." After-dinner coffee in the office, which was once a minor breach of routine, appears now to have become a part of routine. "We had left the dining room and crossed the hall to the office, and Fritz had brought coffee and Wolfe had poured it."

PHYSICAL ASPECTS ::: This tells us something about the neighborhood: "I have often sat there [on the front stoop] watching the neighborhood kids at stoop ball." Archie says the door and the walls of the front room (the specific reference is to the door between the office and the front room, though the implication is that the walls are too) are soundproofed. Archie mentions "the Heron sedan which Wolfe owns and I drive." Finally, Archie says that his desk is at right angles to Wolfe's.

"Eeny Meeny Murder Mo" [January 1959], published in *Homicide Trinity*, 1962.

THE STORY ::: I hope a long quote will be forgiven here, as it says so much and says it so well; besides, it lays the basis for what happens in the tale:

> I was standing there in the office with my hands in my pockets, glaring down at the necktie on Nero Wolfe's desk, when the doorbell rang.
>
> Since it would be a different story, and possibly no story at all, if the necktie hadn't been there, I had better explain about it. It was the one Wolfe had worn that morning--borown silk with little yellow curlicues, a Christmas gift from a former client. At lunch Fritz, coming to remove the leavings of the spareribs and bring the salad and ch-ese, had told Wolfe there was a drop of sauce on his tie, and Wolfe had dabbed at it with his napkin; and later, when we had left the dining room to cross the hall to the office, he had removed the tie and put it on his desk. He can't stand a spot on his clothes, even in private. But he hadn't thought it worth the effort to go up to his room for another one, since no callers were expected, and when four o'clock came and he left for his afternoon session with the orchids in the plant rooms on the roof, his shirt was still unbuttoned at the neck and the tie was still on his desk.
>
> It annoyed me. It annoyed Fritz too when, shortly after four, he came to say he was going shopping and would be gone two hours. His eye caught the tie and fastened on it. His brows went up.
>
> "*Schlampick*," I said.
>
> He nodded. "You know my respect and esteem for him. He has great spirit and character, and of course he is a great detective, but there is a limit to the duties of a chef and housekeeper. One must draw the line somewhere. Besides, there is my arthritis. You haven't got arthritis, Archie."
>
> "Maybe not," I conceded, "but if you rate a limit so do I. My list of functions from confidential assistant detective down to errand boy is a mile long, but it does not include valeting. Arthritis is beside the point. Consider the dignity of man. He could have taken it on his way up to the plant rooms."
>
> "You could put it in a drawer."
>
> "That would be evading the issue."
>
> "I suppose so." He nodded. "I agree. It is a delicate affair. I must be going." He went.

So, when one Bertha Aarons comes to the brownstone without an appointment shortly after five in the afternoon, Archie shows her into the office where Wolfe's tie still lies upon his desk. The case she wishes to engage Wolfe on arises out of marital difficulties, but Archie goes up to the plant rooms to rag Wolfe about taking it anyway, leaving Aarons in the office. When he returns, some twenty minutes later, he finds her lying in the office floor, strangled to death with Wolfe's tie. Wolfe's dignity is affronted, what with the murder taking place in his office and with his tie, and he determines to take his revenge by exposing the killer (for no fee). Involved in the investigation are the several members of the law firm for which Aarons worked and which was involved in the problem about which she wished to consult Wolfe. Wolfe does expose the murderer, though his technique for doing so is hardly worthy of his genius. Indeed, had the murderer remained cool, Wolfe could not have proved anything, at least not with the evidence he had at hand.

WOLFE ::: Archie says, regarding Wolfe's motivation,

> He has made the claim, to me, that the one and only thing that impels him to work is his desire to live in what he calls acceptable circumstances in the old brownstone on West 35th Street, Manhattan, which he owns, with Fritz as chef and Theodore as orchid tender and me as goat (not his word).

But, as we have seen before, there are some things that he will not do: "One of the kinds of jobs Wolfe wouldn't touch, even directly, was divorce stuff." However, with the woman dead with Wolfe's tie around her neck there's just no way he can avoid this one. Indeed, he takes it as a personal affront and determines to lay hands on the villain without even taking a fee:

> "Have you even known me to show rancor?"
> "I'd have to look in the dictionary. What is it exactly?"
> "Vehement ill will. Intense malignity."
> "No."
> "I have it now, and it is in the way. I can't think clearly. I intend to expose that wretch before the police do. . . .
> "This confounded rancor is a pimple on the brain. My mental processes haven't been so muddled in many years."

Again:

> I have no client [this in reply to a question from Cramer]. I am going to aveng an affront to my dignity and self-esteem. . . . I cannot escape the ignominy of having my necktie presented in a courtroom as an exhibit of the prosecution; I may even have to suffer the indignity of being called to the stand to identify it; but I want the satisfaction of exposing the culprit who used it.

In fact, he does not have to attend court to identiry it, but his ordeal is acute, nonetheless:

> Now, after nearly five hours, they were gone, all except Sergeant Purley Stebbins, who was in the office using the phone, and Cramer. Fritz was in the kitchen, on his third bottle of wine, absolutely miserable. Added to the humiliation of a homicide in the house he kept was the incredible fact that Wolfe had passed up a meal. He had refused to eat a bite. Around eight o'clock he had gone up to his room, and Fritz had gone up twice

> with a tray, and he had only snarled at him. When I had gone up
> at 10:30 with a statement for him to sign, and told him they
> were taking the rug [on which the woman's body had lain], he
> made a noise but had no words.

Fritz is still trying to feed Wolfe at two in the morning when Archie enters the office and finds Wolfe and his chef in conversation:

> "No," Wolfe was saying grimly. "You know quite well I almost never eat at night."
> "But you had no dinner. An omlet, or at least--"
> "No! Confound it, let me starve! Go to bed!"
> Fritz looked at me, I shook my head, and he went.

A few familiar items need mentioning:

> Wolfe was leaning back with his eyes closed, his fists on his chair arms, and his mouth working. When he does that with his lips, pushing them out and pulling them in, out and in, he is not to be interrupted, so I crossed to my desk and sat. That can last anywhere from two minutes to half an hour. That time it wasn't much more than two minutes.

Also: "Wolfe refuses to work either his brain or his tongue on business at table." And his weight is given as 270 pounds. Finally, we get to see Wolfe in unusually close contact with a member of the fairer sex:

> There was a combination of sounds from the [office]: a kind of cry or squeal, . . . a sort of scrape or flutter, and what might have been a grunt from Wolfe. I dived for the connecting door and went with it as I swung it open, and kept going, but two paces short of Wolfe's desk I halted to take in a sight I had never seen before and never expected to see again: Nero Wolfe with his arms tight around a beautiful young woman in his lap, pinning her arms, hugging her close to him. I stood paralysed.
> "Archie!" he roared. "Confound it, get her!"

ARCHIE ::: Wolfe says, "You have a flair for dealing with personable young women", to which Archie replies, "Sure. They melt like chocolate bars in the sun."

OTHER REGULARS ::: We learn that Theodore weight 135 pounds. Rowcliff is mentioned, as is Lon Cohen, and Wolfe talks to Nathaniel Parker on the phone. Fritz, who is always present, is a bit more visible in this episode:

> Fritz was in my breakfast chair, humped over with his forehead on the edge of the table.
> "You're pie-eyed," I said.
> His head came up. "No, Archie. I have tried, but no."
> "Go to bed."
> "No. He will be hungry."
> "He may never be hungry again. Pleasant dreams."

Saul, Fred and Orrie are also present, and Archie says having them there costs sixty bucks. (This is odd: Archie does not specify how much time the $60 covers, so it is presumably for a day; but, as the following item demonstrates, $60 would not even cover Saul's wages for a day, much less all three of them). "At the corner I was joined by a little guy with a big nose who looked, at first sight, as if he might make forty bucks a week waxing floors. Actually Saul Panzer was the best operative in the metropolitan area and his rate was ten dollars an hour." And of course Cramer and Purley are on the scene. In fact, Cramer shows up with warrants for the arrest of Wolfe and Archie as material witnesses. Archie says, of Cramer, "His big round face is always redder at night, making his gray hair look whiter." Elsewhere Archie says "I heard the front door close with a bang, so it was Purley. Cramer never banged doors." Archie elaborates on Purley: "There is one thing that would give Purley more pleasure than to take Wolfe or me in, and that would be to take both of us. Wolfe cuffed to him and me cuffed to Wolfe would be perfect."

PHYSICAL ASPECTS ::: There are some interesting items for this section, foremost among them being an explanation of how the brownstone could have windows on the side without being a corner house. Archie goes into the front room, expecting to find a woman he had left there shortly before still there. She wasn't. "Through a wide-open window cold air was streaming in. . . . I went to it and stuck my head out . . . . It was a relief to see that the areaway, eight feet down, was unoccupied." Regarding that front room Archie remarks, "The wall and door are soundproofed." While we are at the front of the house we might note that the chain bolt isn't being used in this episode. "The rack" in the hall is mentioned, though. Moving into the office we learn that there is a thermostat on the office wall, and that it is turned down at night but kept at 70 when there are visitors present. The safe in the office is also mentioned, as is "a big hunk of jade which Wolfe used for a paperweight." And the peephole:

> I returned to the hall [from the office] and turned left, toward the kitchen; and there, in the alcove at the end of the hall, was Wolfe, standing at the hole. The hole was through the wall at eye level. On the office side it was covered by a picture of a waterfall. On this side, in the alcove, it was covered by nothing, and you could not only hear through but also see through.

Archie also mentions "the two-way door to the kitchen." And he says, "I went to the hall, mounted one flight, turned left, tapped on the door, heard a sound that was half growl and half groan, opened the door, and entered [Wolfe's bedroom]." In order to turn left, Archie must have gone up the rear stairs (as I will explain in the far-distant future when I finally get around to doing a full-scale discussion of the layout of the brownstone). Finally, Archie says that one proceeds from the vestibule through the cool room, the tropical room and the intermediate room before arriving at the potting room.

ODDS & ENDS ::: Wolfe asks a man where he was Monday of last week, which was the Monday before New Year's, and the man replies, "I was at the Manhattan Chess Club watching the tournament. Bobby Fischer won his adjourned game with Weinstein in fifty-eight moves." Incidentally, when the case opens "the year was only five days old."

MYSTERY*FILE

SHORT REVIEWS BY STEVE LEWIS

James Crumley, *The Last Good Kiss* (Random House, 1978; 259 pp.).
    Most private eyes work out of huge metropolitan cities like New York, Los Angeles and San Francisco. Through the years a handful of others have based their somewhat seedier operations in midwestern population centers such as Chicago, Cleveland and Indianapolis. On television this season there is an example of how a Las Vegas detective goes about his business, but you'd have to admit that the glamor and glitter of that particular show is far from typical of mainstream America, and so it remains far more reminiscent of that old stand-by of the pulp magazines, the Hollywood private eye story.
    C. W. Sughrue's home is Montana, however, and his outlook on life and happiness, or the pursuit thereof, is correspondingly closer to a segment of American demographics long ignored by other authors, obsessed with the bizarre vagaries of life in southern California, for example.
    Rocky Mountain jade. Sughrue is often dirty and unshaven, and a good deal of the time he's drunk, or close to it, but never obnoxiously so. He's as much a combination of hippie and redneck as either variety of humanity could ever recognize as possible. He mixes affably with both, and yet he has the same moral obligation to himself that all the great private detectives of literature have had to have hidden inside. The story, as it strips his character carefully away in layers, is so intensely revealing that for him to become yet another series creation would be close to pointless.
    The story, as muddled, or even more so, as any in real life, begins with a hunt for a famous bar-hopping poet and novelist who takes him on a binge through several states before he's found, but before he can return home Sughrue is sidetracked into chasing down a runaway girl, lost and not found in the pornographic environs of San Francisco ten years earlier.
    Lives are muddled as well, and revelations are painfully hard to come by. The Tale Crumley has to tell builds slowly and easily into a climax that explodes with all the emotional thrill of a gut-satisfying revenge about to be released.
    Crumley is not the new Hammett. He's closer to Chandler, if names must be dropped, but in several ways he's the equal of both, their peer. In fact, he's that rarity, an authentic rough-hewn original, and they don't happen along very often. (A plus)* (Reviews so marked have appeared earlier in the Hartford *Courant*.)

Jan Roffman, *One Wreath with Love* (Doubleday/ Crime Club, 1978; 184 pp.).
    Jan Roffman has written nearly a dozen mystery novels by now, so it's be exceedingly presumptious of me to try to generalize anything about her writing from a sample of size only one, but I will anyway. She has a tendency to overwrite hideously, especially in the early chapters, and she creates a good many characters whose lives are as ingeniously intertwined as they are in the best tradition of soap opera tragedy.

However, the overwriting does seem to disappear as the characters become more familiar, and by the end tears will come close to falling. Murder is involved, but we know who did it in chapter one, in which a particularly repugnant death scene is needed to build an almost watertight alibi.

Many of the characters are afflicted with various stages of senility or insanity, and maybe that's what I mistook for overwriting. Roffman is clearly superb in creating people out of touch with reality. The contrast is most effective when an underdisciplined seven-year-old named Tilly makes a friend of the dottering old lady who may have caught sight of the killer. There's also the rapidly failing mind of the ex-wife with a not-so-reliable ghost haunting her, and so in turn Chief Superintendent Deacon is annoyed.

This is not a detective story, but all the same, I think it can easily get under your skin. (B plus)

Stephen Whitney, *Singled Out* (Morrow, 1978; 261 pp.).

I can't imagine myself in a singles bar. I hope I'm not classifying myself as a hopeless social misfit with that remark, but I say it to help demonstrate how the crazed killer in this book differs so greatly from Dan Greenberg's psychopath in his recent and structurally very similar *Love Kills*, reviewed here not long ago. David Cooper (we know his name this time) is what you would call a smooth operator, quite capabel of picking up good-looking but unattached career women with an evening on their hands and bringing them home for the loving of their lives--before his hatred for them takes over. In *Love Kills*, it was just the opposite--the killer truly loved his victims, but he was hopelessly inadequate in initiating any kind of personal relationship with them. (And any further inference as to which I identify more closely with is quite clearly out of line.)

Steven Whitney's previous books--this is his first try at fiction--include such titles as *Vincent Price Unmasked*, *Charles Bronson Superstar*, and *It's Your Body: A Woman's Guide to Gynecology*, and of the three, it's probably the last one which was of the most use in writing this one. At times it's not very comfortable reading. David Cooper has a very sick mind.

The response of the NYPD to their growing list of unsolved murders is close to being unique, and if this sort of crime-solving technique has ever been used in practice, it's no wonder it's been hushed up. As bait for the killer, volunteer policewomen are used. And 'used' is the right word. What they're asked to do is hang around various singles bars scattered throughout Manhattan, allow themselves to be picked up by likely-looking suspects and talked into bed. Even with a male partner right outside the door, this does seem to be beyond the call of duty. And of course it causes problems, since policemen and policewomen are only human too.

This is strong adult reading. While it has all the sex and violence that could possibly be objected to, the purpose of this book is not entirely that of titillation. Mixed in with the suspense that makes it nearly impossible to lay this story down is the same sensitivity to life and being that makes so much of today's crime fiction far superior to the artificial plot devices predominant in most of the detective novels from the Golden Age of Mysteries. And this is why I sometimes feel (dare I say it?) that a book like this is worth five or six of those by someone like John Rhode, and at least a dozen of those by a Freeman Wills Crofts. (A)

C. A. Haddad, *The Moroccan* (Harper & Row, 1975; Bantam, 1978; 279 pp.).
   What the ad copy on the front cover would like very much to have you do is to "meet Israel's sexiest superspy". Well, to do that, you have to buy the book, take it home and read it, and that's what they really had in mind. And which I've done. How does it measure up?
   It is true that Judah Biton is an Israeli, but being a 'dark and dangerous' Morrocan, he finds the clash of cultures taking place within the Promised Land working decidedly in the favor of the white European Jew ruling class. He takes a slight revenge upon them by marrying his army sergeant, the daughter of two pig-faced Germans, but as far as his love life is concerned, except for one incident nearly forced upon him, his jewel of a wife is quite enough. And he is one of the most reluctant spies to be in the business. Not very James Bondian, but the approach is honest. Make up your own minds about the cover claims.
   The story, after a hundred pages of domestic travail, involves of course Israel's never-ending struggle with undercover Arab terrorists, who remain ever dangerous, in spite of the continual quarrelsome infighting plaguing their efforts. What benefit the reader gains is a different view of the problems of the Middle East on a level below that which makes headlines. Sorrow has to be felt for all the innocent victims of an unwanted war. (B)

F. Lee Bailey, *Secrets* (Stein & Day, 1978; 253 pp.).
   The whole world may not love a courtroom mystery, but most assuredly there are a lot of us who do. And with the name of this particular author on this one, there's not far wrong we can go in expecting an authentic and suspenseful account of a complicated and juicy murder trial, one capable of attracting national attention. This one has it all, including an attempted mid-Atlantic jet hijacking, an X-rated attic, and more than a dash of Mafioso involvement.
   This is Bailey's first attempt at writing fiction, and there is a corresponding amount of highly overwrought dialogue, but you can't help but feel that there's a healthy amount of Mr. Bailey himself in each of the several lawyers and attorneys working so diligently for the defense. Their job is to keep famous criminal attorney Michael Kilrayne from serving a lifetime sentence in prison, in spite of the fact that the body of the supposed victim has never been found. Even though the charges are obviously trumped up and motivated by political resentments and purely personal hatreds, the danger is real enough.
   Much of the action takes place outside the courtroom, and a great deal of fascinating per-trial maneuvering goes on, but skirting some touchy matters of professional ethics, the case remains as it should, in the hands of the jury. (B plus)

Franklin Bandy, *Deceit and Deadly Lies* (Charter, 1978; 403 pp.).
   It's awfully hard to sink $2.25 into a paperback original writen by someone you've never heard of before. If you have

book opens with an impressive bit of bluff-calling that closes out a 'friendly' game of poker. (2) The dead man with a solidly satisfying marriage to a wife in San Francisco is not totally immune to playing a role with the starlet beauties of Los Angeles. (3) One of the starlets gets pregnant on cue, and she calls upon the widow for assistance.

A long and complicated detective story develops, but I fear that it's too much of the former for its own good. The plot mixes the usual ingredients with some freshness; the writing is only adequate. (C plus)

Robert Terrall, *Sand Dollars* (St. Martin's, 1978; 347 pp.).

There's a lot of money floating around this world that most of us never get the slightest glimpse of. Tax shelters for the rich being in high demand, a great deal of this money accumulates in out-of-the-way places like regulation-free Grand Cayman Island. When the mild-mannered accountant who first discovered this Caribbean financial paradise turns down the Mafia as a silent partner in his operations, he's forced to turn to bank robbery in retaliation and as a means for sheer survival. What results is a lusty tale of greed and marital infidelity, spiced with numerous feats of sexual superheroism. Unfortunately none of the hapless, amoral creatures involved arouse much sympathy when things don't work out quite as planned, and at length the story crumbles into what's left of sand castles when the tide comes inevitably in. (C)

Michael Allen, *Spence and the Holiday Murders* (Walker, 1977; first U.S. publication 1978; 173 pp.).

The season is Christmas, the victim is a swinging young bachelor with an unsuspected habit of snapping photos through the windows of the girls' school across the way, and so the immediate conclusion is that someone was being blackmailed.

As everyone has come to expect of the British police procedural, Detective Superintendent Spence's investigation is carried out so diligently and smoothly that it could as well serve as a primer for the novice mystery reader. (C plus)

Thomas Gifford, *The Glendower Legacy* (Putnam's, 1978; 321 pp.).

The academic world scores a couple of telling blows to the ungodly in this, the latest thriller to come from the typewriter of the author of the highly acclaimed *The Wind Chill Factor*, but otherwise not all is well.

To borrow a term from the incomparable Mr. Hitchcock of movie fame, the MacGuffin, the object that all parties devoutly desire but which in fact may be all that keeps the plot moving, is a document dating from the days of the American Revolution--from Valley Forge, to be precise, at a time when morale was low and the ravages of dysentery were visibly high. Betrayal at any moment, even by the commander-in-chief himself, given the right conditions and frame of mind, was an ever-present possibility.

If this document could be authenticated, the resulting scandal would rock the nation, and a director of the Russian KGB with a sense of humor takes a serious interest as well. The scene shifts dramatically to Harvard Square and then to the remotest crannies of Maine before heading even further north, to a massive house located high up on the rocks of the any doubts at all, even an enthusiastic quote on the cover by Thomas Chastain ("James Bond as he might have been conceived by Lawrence Sanders") probably won't do much to convince you. Chastain has said it well, however, and if by any chance you've been waiting for my opinion, I'd say it's worth your money.

The cover also says that this is a novel of detection, assassination and suspense, but what that has to do with the tradition of *The Spy Who Came in from the Cold* is greatly subject to conjecture. Bandy has a good many pages to work with, and a large portion of the story he tells is slow, leisurely and discursive, filled with what some might call homespun philosophy, about what having the powers of a god, even in part, can do to a man.

The hero is Kevin MacInnes, a retired army colonel who's making a new career for himself. His means to new fame and fortune is a little black box, a Psychological Stress Evaluator, more powerful at detecting lies from voice analysis than any other sort of polygraph ever devised. Men in position and power flock to MacInnes for his services, and so it's no great wonder that he begins to get the feeling that he's judge and jury wrapped into one. Until he begins to make mistakes, that is, of the kind that cost men lives . . . .

Keeping the story from going off in too many directions, there really is a political assassination about to take place, and plenty of blood flows in the final few chapters. Here's where the advertised suspense comes in, but if this were all the story was about, it's be just another thriller. Bandy gets high marks this time because he can tell a story and because he has something else to say. He's worth watching for again. (A minus)

POSTSCRIPT: Al Hubin's long awaited *Bibliography of Crime Fiction* is finished and has just arrived. It seems that Bandy is (was) also Eugene Franklin, who wrote a handful of 'Berkley Barnes' stories a number of years back. Another book under the Bandy by-line is *The Shannonese Hustle,* just out from Avon, about karate, dope and belly-dancers. Maybe it's better than it sounds.

Elmore Leonard, *The Switch* (Bantam, 1978; 216 pp.).

Two ex-cons named Ordell and Louis, obviously too refined to be winners in a Cheech and Chong look-alike contest, kidnap a suburban Detroit housewife, a tennis mother named Mickey, whose husband Frank is a crooked contractor and secretly planning on leaving her and skipping off to the Caribbean. Not surprisingly, he quite happily ignores the ransom demands, sending their dreams of a cool million disappearing upwards in clouds of thin, billowing smoke.

Detroit's not a very nice city, and Leonard knows it and tells it. But while the ending of his story comes as a subtle sort of surprise, the looseness with which he establishes it pretty much undermines the effect. The Dawsons' marriage is as shaky from the start. (C plus)

David Anthony, *Stud Game* (Pocket, 1978, 256 pp.).

I like mysteries that have titles with two meanings, but believe it or not, this one has three! (1) Stan Bass, who for a friend undertakes a job normally performed by private detectives, is in his own words by profession a gambler. The stern Nova Scotia coast.

The hero, taking the role that Cary Grant would play, is a native, middle-aged professor of American history, and when he takes refuge in the home of the fiercely liberated tv newsperson (Audrey Hepburn) in spite of their initial mutual antagonisms, you know that everything is just going to be all right. Harvard, however, will hardly be the same. Bodies pile up, torture scenes (with pliers) abound--and for what?

Successful combinations of comedy, blood and suspense can be done. They are a specialty of the Mr. Hitchcock previously referred to. Gifford can weave a nasty spell with words, but the enormous improbability of such a sequence of events, given the timetable suggested, drags the early part of the story into a puzzling morass of page-flipping, and the jagged abruptness with which it's all wrapped up in shiny paper only points out the lack of solid substance throughout. Nothing is gained. Pessimistically, some worthwhile lives are lost, and the joke can't be maintained forever.

Definitely written with the movies in mind, that much should have been made clear, and it could very well make a good one: it's flashy and glib, and the weaknesses in the foundation can be easily overlooked. After the excitement dies down, as it most definitely will, the sugar-coating is immediately recognized. Artificial, and not very satisfying. (C plus)*

Michael Underwood, *Crooked Wood* (St. Martin's, 1978; 191 pp.).

Mystery stories usually end where this one begins, with the murderer safely behind bars and about to stand trial. Underwood's forte is the courtroom drama, British style, and here the problem is twofold: who hired the contract killer who actually did the job, and who's trying to buy off one of the jurors? Sergeant Atwell's work is clearly not done, and it requires the timely assistance of his ex-policewoman wife and the gathering in of an overabundant supply of red herrings before a surprise Mr. X is named. A deftly woven detective tale it is, and an interesting variation from the norm. (B)

Leslie Egan, *Look Back on Death* (Doubleday/Crime Club, 1978; 183 pp.).

Lawyer Jesse Falkenstein's preoccupation with parapsychology is evident from page one on. Confirmed skeptics of ESP, clairvoyance, and mediums who can contact spirits of the dead are warned that while this case of murder which occurred eight years before does contain a good deal of detection via exhaustive legwork, the source of the final clue is sure to irritate their sensitive sensibilities more than a little. Egan, who also writes the Dell Shannon books, otherwise does her usual fine job with dialogue and sharp characterization. (B)

Erica Quest, *The Silver Castle* (Doubleday/Crime Club, 1978; 188 pp.).

The discovery that Gail Sherbrooke's father, who she'd thought dead for over twenty years, had just committed suicide in Switzerland sends the aspiring young artist off on a search to learn the truth about a man she had never known.

Lying just beyond her reach she finds both mystery and romance--the type of story most readers surely find done far too often, and rather badly, too. That's not at all the case here. With much of the charm and intricacy of a hand-made Swiss clock, this is indeed an uncluttered detective story that's both haunting and wholly enchanting. (B)*

Judson Philips, *A Murder Arranged* (Dodd Mead, 1978; 183 pp.).
    Journalist Peter Styles' crusade against senseless violence leads him to an out-of-the-way New England village where he becomes the champion of a young man accused and convicted of murder. All the evidence seems to point directly to Tim Ryan, but the feeling of at least half the townspeople is that the state police wrapped up their case far too quickly.
    Obviously there's more than a little resemblance here to a story that recently made Connecticut headlines, and the reader is swallowed up at once into the affairs of a small town. In spite of some fast deductions and the long arm of coincidence in the final chapters, Philips demonstrates once again that few authors are so non-stop reliable as he. (B minus)

Robert B. Parker, *The Judas Goat* (Houghton Mifflin, 1978; 181 pp.).
    Another book in the hard-boiled Spenser series is always more than welcome. *Promised Land*, the one just preceding this one, won a great deal of critical acclaim, including an Edgar award, but in spite of extraordinarily good writing, it was noticeably thin on plot, and in many ways it was largely an introspective character study of the tough Boston private eye named Spenser, and the world around him.
    As if to compensate, this time the pace is fast and bloody, regenerating the series completely by means of extreme violence. A gang of terrorists wipes out most of a wealthy industrialist's family, and Spenser is hired to track them down. After a cleansing process of this ferocity, digging out those responsible, we can only look forward to what's in store for the future--and, no, Spenser's proven that he's not yet too old for this sort of thing.
    Not a perfect book, but then again, so few are. (A)

Charles L. Grant, *The Sound of Midnight* (Doubleday, 1978; 179 pp.).
    If Mr. Grant has his way, the small New England village of Oxrun Station will soon have a reputation to rival those of the famous towns a certain Mr. Lovecraft wrote so often about. This latest mystery that overtakes a handful of its inhabitants begins with the precocious behavior of some ordinary schoolchildren and quickly grows to nightmarish proportions as some forgotten misanthropic gods of Celtic mythology struggle to bring their evil forces back into the world.
    One way of producing the uneasy feeling that things are happening that are vaguely unright is to utilize the sort of murky overwriting that Grant uses here, but maybe it's time to wonder if sharp, clean prose might not get the job done just as efficiently. There are some chilling moments here, but unfortunately too few of them strike home deeply enough to be truly memorable. (B minus)

P. M. Hubbard, *The Quiet River* (Doubleday/Crime Club, 1978; 181 pp.).
    In moving from London to the country one knows there will be unforeseen adjustments to be made, but one hardly expects

the presence of a nearby river to become a mysteriously sinister threat to the happiness of a young couple like the Andersons. Yet, with the underlying support of the dourly aloof farmer who works the land along its banks, even their marriage crumbles against its force. A great deal of inner turmoil inevitably burbles over, with every phrase of conversation and each possible interpretation being minutely scrutinized. Like water that creeps ever chinward in a room with neither doors nor windows, this hypnotically haunting story will both chill and terrify. (A)

Jack Foxx, *Wildfire* (Bobbs-Merrill, 1978; 233 pp.).
   A drought-stricken and dried up corner of northern California, an ultra-conservative logging baron with an illegal stockpile of guns and ammunition, and a marriage in trouble-- all waiting for the right spark to set them off. There's only one way out, and that's by taking one of the most hair-raising train rides you've ever been on, travelling by antique steam locomotive through a countryside going up in flames. Even second-hand, this is without a doubt one trip you won't want to be left behind on. (A)

Lawrence Block, *The Burglar in the Closet* (Random House, 1978; 166 pp.).
   In *Burglars Can't Be Choosers*, when last we met our favorite breaking-and-entering expert, Bernie Rhodenbarr, he was nabbed red-handed in an apartment which, quite unknown to him, came complete with a corpse in the bedroom. This time, he checks around first. While the murder's being committed, he finds himself accidentally locked up in a closet instead. The victim, no one important, only his dentist's not-so-favorite ex-wife.
   So, in the midst of the comedy routines provided for by dentistry and other irreverent views of the world, Bernie is forced once again to become a detective on the run--burglars find it terribly difficult to get policemen to be sympathetic to their job-related problems. The end result is fast, fresh, breezy, and wow, was I slow on the clues! (B plus)

Ruth Rendell, *A Sleeping Life* (Doubleday, 1978; 180 pp.).
   Chief Inspector Wexford's approach to a murder is often based on intuition rather than fact, but this time, working on the death of a middle-aged woman with no trace of background, he seems to run into stone walls in all directions. Adding to his frustration is a domestic crisis at home as well, provoked by his daughter's evangelical conversion to Women's Lib.
   Rendell obviously intends for the ending to come as quite a surprise, but unfortunately it's too great a secret to keep very well, and as a result all the clues end up pointing in only one direction. Even so, the workpersonship* is definitely the solid sort of construction that mystery readers have come to expect of one of today's best mystery writers. There's no reason they should be disappointed this time. (B)
   *Sorry about that.

David S. Lifson, *Headless Victory* (A.S. Barnes, 1978; 178 pp.).
   Since the feature attraction here is the act of recapturing for the summer stage a theatrical scandal involving three

members of the present company, a more accurate, but somewhat less elegant title might well have been that of one of the chapters, "Passions Spin the Plot." Even without the threatening note received by the director as production gets under way, bringing an emotional drama of this sort back out into the open for all forms of amateur hit-and-run psychoanalysis in manifestly asking for trouble.

A hint of lingering McCarthyism (at this late date?) also mars the fine in-depth look Lifson gives us of the internal workings of the creative theatre, pondering as he does so the problem of its survival in this age of ever-escalating costs. As a mystery novel, you can probably do better; the murder finally occurs with but 30 pages to go, and it's solved within the chapter. (C minus)

Bartholomew Gill, *McGarr on the Cliffs of Moher* (Scribner's, 1978; 246 pp.).

Quite remarkably, when three young people from the same small village in County Clare, Ireland, come to New York City, they find nearly equal amounts of success. When it happens that they all return home at the same time, their troubles and their angers are brought with them, and one, the girl reporter after the truth about the IRA, does, stabbed to d-ath with a pitchfork at a lovely spot overlooking the sea.

McGarr is Ireland's top cop. Why he's on this case from the beginning is never made clear. And with background of this sort assumed and/or never properly filled in, and with the failure of McGarr to investigate immediately the questions the reader wants asked (well, you should), it's no wonder that the feeling persists that the mystery is incidental.

What we do have is a very Irish, very picturesque novel about the problems troubling Ireland today. As a worthy reflection on the objectives that the IRA should have (and doesn't), you probably cannot do better. I wish that I had found it more interesting, but I am nearly ashamed to say that I did not. (C minus)

Nora Barry, *Sherbourne's Folly* (Doubleday/Crime Club, 1978; 184 pp.).

The illness of an older sister calls a woman and her adopted daughter back to England from the American suburb where they now live. Once there, as outsiders to the very much ingrown group of relatives and friends left behind, they're forcibly made more and more aware that something sinister and evil is eating away beneath the strained welcome that greets them.

In spite of the obvious Gothic trimmings, the accent on time, memory and the nostalgia for a vanished childhood makes this a refreshing change of pace from the hard-boiled violence, for example, of a tale told by a tough private eye. It's a must as well for lovers of treasure hunts, mazes, and yes, even mansions with secret passages. (B minus)*

VERDICT
(More Reviews)

Ellery Queen, ed., *The Misadventures of Sherlock Holmes* (Little, Brown, 1944).

The Misadventures of Sherlock Holmes, a much sought after collection of Sherlockian parodies and pastiches, was published by Little Brown & Co. in March, 1944, and reprinted in April, 1944. A special edition of approximately 125 copies was distributed at the 1944 Baker Street Irregulars Dinner. The value of a copy of this prized volume today can vary from $40.00 to $150.00 depending on the edition and condition of the book. Of course, the value of one of the special editions presented to The Baker Street Irregulars would be substantially higher.

The contents of the book fary from reverent parodies to sheer farce, but all were obviously written with a great deal of respect for the original Holmes stories. Most of the stories and pastiches were originally published in magazines such as *Punch* or *Puck* or in anthologies. A few, such as "The Mary Queen of Scots Jewel" by William O. Fuller and "The Unique Hamlet" by Vincent Starret were previously printed only in private editions in very small numbers. And at least one, "The Adventure of the Illustrious Impostor" by Anthony Boucher makes its first appearance anywhere in this prestigious volume.

In the introduction Frederick Dannay tells of his childhood introduction to the remarkable Sherlock Holmes. With pangs of nostalgia, which bring to the reader's mind his or her own discovery of the tales of The Great Master, Dannay reveals how a painful ear infection was relieved by the diverting adventures of Sherlock Holmes and Watson. Dannay and Manfred Lee join in telling the whys and wherefores of the selection of stories which comprise the volume, listing those pastiches considered inappropriate and those which deserved honorable mention.

The table of contents reads like a Who's Who in literature--Maurice Leblanc, Anthony Berkeley, Agatha Christie, Mark Twain, Bret Harte, O. Henry, J. Kendrick Bangs, August Derleth, 33 stories in all, by 31 different authors.

The parody contributed by Carolyn Wells is perhaps the most irreverent of the lot. Entitled "The Adventures of the Clothes-line," the story first appeared in *The Century*, May, 1915. Sherlock Holmes, the President of The Society of Infallible Detectives, leads his fellow club members on a merry deductive and inductive chase trying to deduce why a beautiful young woman dressed in an evening gown and dazzling jewelry was hanging by her hands from a clothes-line suspended between two tenement houses. Vidocq, Arsene Lupin, The Thinking Machine, Raffles, Lecoq, Mr. Gryce, Rouletabille, and Scientific Sprague all have their turn with hilarious results, but to no avail. Holmes negates their theories with his own solution, "The lady thought she heard a mouse, so she scrambled out of the window, preferring to risk her life on the perilous clothes-line rather than stay in the dwelling where the mouse was also." However the chief of police disagrees and Watson, as usual, has the last word.

Anthony Berkeley's parody is outrageous but wonderfully witty. Imagine a Holmes story done in the style of P.G. Wodehouse. Watson becomes a most proper Jeeves and Holmes is a lady-chasing man about town. "What Ho!"

The most popular take-off on Holmes' unique powers of observation appears to be his ability to read a man's name from his hatband. This particular gimmick is repeated in no less than four stories. Allusions to Holmes' habit of indulging in the use of cocaine are also abundant.

Ironically, considering the missing lady episode of her own life, Agatha Christie's parody is entitled "The Case of the Missing Lady." A woman who has been engaged for two years is found to be missing when her fiance returns home from an exploring expedition two weeks early. Tommy and Tuppence, doing an imitation of Holmes and Watson, try to search out the missing lady only to find out that the solution must not be revealed.

In Stephen Leacock's "Maddened by Mystery" or The Defective, Sherlock Holmes' masterful means of disguise is utilized to the fullest as he wins first prize in the international dog show.

In Bret Harte's "The Stolen Cigar Case" Holmes and Watson are irreversibly alienated by an exaggeration of Holmes' paranoia, and a misuse of circumstantial evidence.

August Derleth's "The Adventure of the Norcross Riddle" is, in my opinion, truest to the form of the original Holmes stories. Although Holmes is now Solar Pons and Dr. Watson becomes Dr. Parker, the narrative reads much like a Doyle tale, starting with a visitor who has a perplexing problem of a delicate nature, followed by an investigative excursion by Pons and Parker, the solution of the puzzle, and the capture of the culprits left to the police.

My own favorite selection is "Christmas Eve" by S.C. Roberts. Written in the form of a play, it was originally published as a private edition of 100 copies. It shows a touching, human side of Sherlock Holmes and a wonderfully warm interaction between Mrs. Hudson and Holmes with Dr. Watson the ultimate hero. In addition to the delightful parodies and pastiches, *The Misadventures of Sherlock Holmes* contains extremely interesting and informative introductions to each piece, cleverly provided by Ellery Queen to help the reader place the story in perspective to the times in which it was written and the career of the person who wrote the story.

For the avid Sherlockian who can never get enough, there is a five page bibliography at the end of the book which lists many other gems for which he may search. (Mary Ann Grochowski)

Kingsley Amis, *The Riverside Villas Murder* (Harcourt-Brace-Jovanovich, 1973).

This book, copyrighted 1973, and printed (I would guess) from two to four years later in the U.S. by Harcourt-Brace-Jovanovich, was a conscious attempt to "recapture the rapture" of classic, polite British mysteries. The author is known primarily for his very successful first novel, *Lucky Jim*, his criticism and editing in the science fiction field, and his connection with James Bond. The latter, with the best book of Bond criticism (*The James Bond Dossier*) and the only post-Fleming authorized Bond adventure (the pseudonymous *Col. Sun*), would suggest that this particular writer might be better equipped than most to recreate an antiquarian form that he (and many of us) loved.

The book *is* largely a success, and even its failings are of interest. It is highly recommended, and with what reservations will become apparent as you continue to read this review. First, a warning. Sex is the motive for the murder, and the main point of view character does some homosexual experimenting (which is not graphically presented) as he passes through adolescence.

The murder is ingenious to a fault, and preceded by an apparently unrelated crime that is even more bizarre, but which turns out to be related to the murder, after all. The chief detective, a rural British Acting Chief Constable, is as satisfactorily eccentric and cratchety as any detective out of Christie, Carr or even Poe. He refuses to allow Scotland Yard to help with his investigation, he constantly pooh-poohs such standard techniques as fingerprinting and questioning/seeking possible witnesses, he cheerfully browbeats most witnesses and all his underlings, and he steeps himself in the works of the polite mystery writers.

Point of view is fragmented among several characters, but handled with Amis's usual skill. However, this technique brings out one of the major faults; the author has coupled his fine tale of deduction and wits-matching with a rather conventional (at least in the 1970s) "story of initiation". One important character, integral to the plot as son of one suspect and closely associated with some others, and he is even the one who performs a rather unexpected capture of the guilty party, is searching for identity (sexual and otherwise) as he passes through adolescence. His personal story would not be out of place in a soap opera, or in the kind of modern novel that Dean Koontz calls "big porn", but it is definitely out of place in any sort of mystery. Perhaps this is Amis's way of "updating" his traditional materials, perhaps he did it for shock value, or possibly for some reason that only a critic as sophisticated as Amis himself might be able to guess. For whatever reasons, I (and, I think, most mystery fans will agree) find it a weakness.

The characters are nicely varied and well-drawn, something that has always been one of Amis's strongpoints. The guilty party will probably not be who you think--I was fooled --and may win more than a little of your sympathy. You may well be bothered by the, often unnecessary seeming, changing of focal character. All things considered, I liked it better than *Col. Sun* or *The Anti-Death League*, both of which I also thought worth my reading time. (Jeff Banks)

Richard Neely, *A Madness of the Heart* (Crowell, 1976; Signet, 1977).

Richard Neely specializes in the novel in which nothing is what it seems. This book is no exception. It tells of Harry Falcon, who saves a girl from rape only to return to his home and find his own wife (just released from a sanitarium) raped and beaten. As a rapist begins to terrorize the city, Harry becomes obsessed with finding him and extracting vengeance. In the course of things he meets his childhood sweetheart, and their romance is rekindled; but as he recalls their past love, we learn some strange things about Harry Falcon. Everything falls into place in the end, and the reader begins to see how cleverly Neely has planted little hints all along. Events and phrases take on new meanings as the truth is revealed.

This is a suspense story which carries you right along. The shocking ending might not be as great a surprise to readers of certain detective novelists as it will be to others, but it's a strong one nevertheless. (Bill Crider)

Mark Denning, *Beyond the Prize* (Jove, 1978).
This is the third book of a series featuring John Marshall, the one-armed secret agent (not to be confused with Dan Fortune, the one-armed private eye. This time Marshall is after an AWOL colleague in Ireland, where he tangles with the IRA, the KGB, and just about everyone else. There's plenty of action, plus a plot twist or two that you don't really expect in such an action-oriented story, and Marshall has an enjoyable toughness. There aren't too many books of just this kind being written today, and if you liked James Bond, give it a try. (Bill Crider)

Douglas Rutherford, *Kick Start* (Walker, 1973; Ballantine, 1976).
The hero of this book is really not a person; it's a motorcycle, a Norton Commando to be precise. And while reading the story isn't as much fun as being able to ride as well as the protagonist does, it's a close second.

Kroll commits a crime, gets caught, and is recruited to penetrate an area ravaged by earthquake, accessible only to a skilled biker. He narrowly gets to his destination (a particularly good scene has him crossing a cracking dam), and then things get worse (the dam breaks; the race in front of the flood waters is another high point).

One of the most entertaining things about the book, though, is the large number of flaws in the plot--or what appear to be flaws. The reader keeps thinking that the author is doing a really sloppy job, right up until the end, when suddenly the flaws are shown to be in Kroll's interpretation of events. He's been wrong all along; the reader has been right. And the bitterly ironic ending somehow seems highly appropriate. (Bill Crider)

Chris Steinbrunner and Norman Michaels, *The Films of Sherlock Holmes* (Citadel Press, 253 pp., $14.95).
When will it all end? Are spinoffs on the Sherlock Holmes legend destined to be the one major growth industry not listed on the American Stock Exchange? The answer to the first question is, I hope, "never," not when there are still books to be published that are as good as *The Films of Sherlock Holmes*.

Having collaborated with Mr. Steinbrunner in the past, I was not surprised at his knowledge of Sherlockiana. He has a collaborator in Mr. Michaels whose credentials as a Holmes scholar appear to be equally excellent. For example, when the screen writers of 1933's *A Study in Scarlet* introduce a character named "Jabez Wilson," the authors immediately identify him as coming from a different Doyle story.

Steinbrunner and Michaels cover every film about the Great Detective from one done in 1900 to date of publication in 1978. They even refer to 1979's *Murder by Decree*, released after this book. There is information about the cast of each film, the circumstances of the filming, a description (sometimes too long) of the plot, and a penetrating critique. There are remarkably few errors, though it must be pointed out that *The Seven-Per-Cent Solution* was filmed in 1976, not 1970. While I cavil, I must also note that some captions to the many excellent film stills are silly without being funny and set the wrong tone for a book that is a scholarly, definitive work--as well as an enjoyable one. One caption to a picture from *The Scarlet Claw* (1944) complains that a publicity still "gave away" the identity of the murderer--and then proceeds to do so itself.

Using films in the broadest sense, the authors have included a chapter on television treatments of Holmes. Here they have opted to give the readers as much information as possible. Thus, they have included mysteries which are only tangentially about Holmes--e.g., the television version of Hugh Pentecost's "My Dear Uncle Sherlock" which is not about Holmes but rather is a story about that author's series character, Uncle George Crowder.

Trivia buffs will have a ball with this book, receiving the answers to such questions as:
1. Who played both Holmes *and* Watson; Holmes *and* Raffles; Holmes *and* Philo Vance; Sherlock *and* Mycroft Holmes; Moriarty *and* Inspector Lestrade?
2. In what film was Holmes engaged to be married?
3. What Holmes film used a similar idea as *And Then There Were None*, six years before Agatha Christie?

In size and style this is a "coffee-table" book, but it is one which is not merely for show. It will be referred to too often to ever gather dust. (Marvin Lachman)

Robert Bloch, *Such Stuff as Screams Are Made Of*, introduction by Gahan Wilson (Ballantine/Del Rey, 1979, 283 pp., $1.75).

Although the book is billed as "horror" by the publisher, Bloch disclaims this classification in his afterword, preferring "psychological suspense," and thus enabling the book to fall within the mystery genre. Five of the twenty-one stories herein were first published in mystery magazines (not only EQMM and AHMM, but such pulps as *New Detective* and *15 Mystery Story Magazine*) and another four were first published in men's magazines.

Those who read *The King of Terrors* can expect more of the same here. Bloch specialises in quick bits of horror interspersed with bad puns, as the title shows. It is an understated sort of shock Bloch presents, and as such is well worth reading. A good collection. (B-) (Martin M. Wooster)

Irving Wallace, *The Pigeon Project* (Simon and Schuster, 1979, 383 pp., $10.95).

The latest novel from the bestseller author most loved by students of popular culture. Davis Macdonald discovers a formula for increasing the life span to 150, and sneaks it out of Russia one step ahead of the KGB. He flies to Venice, where he is trapped by the Italian Communists, who do a thorough job of cordoning off the city. Aided by stalwart American publicist Tim Jordan, Macdonald escapes from an Armenian monastery, and spends the remainder of the book plotting how to get out of Venice.

This is a suspense novel with traces of sf. As suspense, it's pretty good. As melodrama, Wallace seems to have been reading his critics too often; one sees various characters being greedy, noble, sacrificial, &c. if almost on cue. Fast, friendly, and forgettable. (B) (Martin Morse Wooster)

Michael Kurland, *The Infernal Device* (Signet, 1978, 251 pp.).

Professor Moriarty saved us all!

At least that's Michael Kurland's report in *The Infernal Device*, a new departure from the Holmes and Holmes influenced stories. *The Infernal Device* deals with the truth behind that diabolical mastermind, the so called Napoleon of Crime, Professor James Moriarty.

It seems that the Russians--even then--were menacing not only The Empire, but all of the freeworld, with their nefarious schemes and dastardly deeds. This particular case in which Holmes is involved, peripherally at least, is no exception.

But even before Holmes is involved in the case, the government of England has sought the aid of none other than the greatest mastermind of them all, James Moriarty. Of course, Moriarty is so clever, that all though it is well known that he is the mastermind behind considerable wrong doing, there is no proof. But this, or so sees the Empire, is the edge. A master criminal against a master criminal. Moriarty against that Russian fiend, Trepoff.

And terror of terrors, Trepoff is such a fiend, it takes the (gulp) unbelievable to stop him. The uniting of the greatest minds in Europe. The teaming of none other than Moriarty and Sherlock Holmes.

Ain't that a corker.

Frankly, I for one, don't believe a word of it. Moriarty is not a nice guy. Not even for money. Shame, shame, shame on Kurland for telling these lies.

But it is an interesting, if a bit over long, book, and worth the 1.95 paper back price. (B) (Joe R. Lansdale)

Stephen Ransome, *The Unspeakable* (Doubleday, 1960; Permabooks, 1962).

John Kirk, a noted photographer recovering from a nervous breakdown, returns to his hometown of Pennswick, in Bucks County, Pennsylvania to recuperate. Avoiding his old friends, he lives reclusively.

Partly because of this, when a five-year-old girl disappears from the neighborhood in which Kirk is living, he comes under the immediate suspicion of police Sergeant Burnett. When Kirk refuses to offer an alibi, Burnett's suspicion hardens into certainty.

Kirk has an alibi, but it's not one he can use. A chance meeting with a girl to whom he once contemplated marriage leads to a tryst in the park which lasted until well after the time of the child's disappearance. But the woman is now Burnett's wife, and Kirk finds himself pulled in several directions.

The Unspeakable is fast-moving and suspenseful; in addition, it is a considerable study of human interaction and emotion in a small town. The story, which is told from several viewpoints, gives us vivid portraits of Kirk, Sgt. Burnett, Laury Burnett, the town's police chief, and several neighbors. That of Sgt. Burnett as a man driven by ambition and certainty of Kirk's guilt to the point of madness is especially vivid.

There is little real detection done here--and the end of the case is brought about by the setting of a trap instead of by deductive thinking. But as a suspense story, *The Unspeakable* is well worth reading. (Gary Crews)

George Alec Effinger, *Felicia* (Berkley, 1978; $1.75).

Arbier, Louisiana, with an estimated population of 3,000, principally Cajuns, descendants of the original settlers, is not unlike other small towns around the country.

It has no police department; the sheriff of the parish and his deputies patrol the town. The sheriff is well liked, a capable and reliable officer, who enjoys his work, with a wife who is dissatisfied, promiscuous, and searching for something she cannot explain.

The television station employs a weather forecaster, a man who cannot get by without his daily dose of "uppers" and "downers". His wife is an unhappy, insecure person who loses sight of reality in the television fantasies she watches daily.

There is the man from Ohio, who ran away from his marriage and his home in desperation, only to find the same frustrations here, and who becomes involuntarily involved with a gang of looters waiting to rob the town.

To all these people will come a memorable experience--the hurricane called "Felicia". The lives of the people, the habits of the Cajuns make interesting reading but the book is also a suspenseful story. (Mrytis Broset)

Douglas Clark, *Deadly Pattern* (Cassell, 1970; Stein & Day, 1970).

In this plodding and drearily written quasi-procedural, the slightly snobbish Detective Chief Inspector George Masters and his three Scotland Yard subordinates are dispatched to a tiny English coastal town to investigate the almost simultaneous disappearances of five drab middle-class women. When four of them are found buried by the seashore, Masters and company crawl into action, taking 169 pages to uncover a psychotic killer who should be apparent to every reader by page 30. A few deft touches of character and description don't save this mediocre tale. (Francis M. Nevins, Jr.)

Clyde B. Clason, *Murder Gone Minoan* (Doubleday, 1939; British title: *Clue to the Labyrinth*, Heinemann, 1939).

This one takes place on a private island off the California coast, owned by a Greek-American department store tycoon with a passion for the ancient Cretan civilization--an ideal setting for an investigation by Theocritus Lucius Westborough, professor of classics and maateur of crime. When a priceless Minoan religious image disappears from the tycoon's Knossos-like palace, Westborough is asked to take the case and soon encounters a mess of amorous intrigues and two murders apparently committed by a worshipper of the snake goddess of Crete. The unusual setting justifies Clason's abundance of classical allusions, and the sections of the story he tells in transcript and document form are neatly handled, but the plot turns out to be a routine matter of professional criminality and Westborough's solution is hopelessly unfair to the reader. A morass of needless adjectives and circumlocutions for "he said" clutter up the ersatz-classical style beyond endurance. (Francis M. Nevins, Jr.)

Robert Portner Koehler, *The Hooded Vulture Murders* (Phoenix, 1947).

Our heroes are two hapless California private eyes who stumble upon the murder of a blackmailing journalist while driving through southern Mexico on the uncompleted Pan American Highway. Naturally the bumbling native officials welcome with open arms the intrusion of two brilliant Anglo sleuths into the case, although the readers may wish the boys had stayed home. Koehler paints local color vividly, but his novel is ineptly plotted, woefully written, pathetically characterized, laughably clued, and all in all a pretty lame excuse for a detective story. (Francis M. Nevins, Jr.)

David Linzee, *Discretion* (Seaview Books, $8.95).

St. Louis' newest mystery novelist is 26-year-old David Linzee, who plots trickily, writes at his best with cinematic vividness, and has a special talent for creating likable unaggressive characters. His first novel, *Death in Connecticut* (1977), was reminiscent of *The Catcher in the Rye* and *The Graduate* and Woody Allen's movies, but his second offers us a merry romp across Europe in the manner of the gentler suspense films of Alfred Hitchcock.

Our tour guides are Sarah Saber, bright young sophisticate and crack shot, and Chris Rockwell, bearish, bearded and the very antithesis of a tough guy. Sarah and Chris are not only lovers but private detectives, and their employer is Inquiries, Incorporated (Inkwink), a computerized agency which is part of a conglomerate of service companies. Descretion is the byword at Inkwink--to such an extent that no one in the organization knows what anyone else is working on.

When an aristocratic french connoisseur decides to keep for himself a priceless Fragonard paintain that he has restored for a Rome museum, he devises a plan that includes having an accomplice impersonate the museum's director and hire Inkwink to send an agent to Rome and test the gallery's security system by trying to steal the painting. The person assigned to this mission is Sarah and she pulls off the theft neatly, but then the real museum officials hire Inkwink to send someone to Rome to investigate the theft, and the operative chosen for this assignment is none other than Chris. And thanks to the policy of discretion, neither detective has any idea that his adversary is the other.

Most of the book is an arily entertaining game of cat-and-mouse, spiced with ridicule aimed both at the super-efficient American corporation and the incompetent Italian bureaucracy. Linzee saves his most spectacular scene for the climax, which takes place in an empty French chateau during a son et lumiere performance.

Those who love the lighter Hitchcock films like "To Catch a Thief" will find that tone and mood perfectly captured in this novel, whose central characters and organization are interesting enough for any number of adventures to come. (Francis M. Nevins, Jr. Reprinted from the St. Louis *Globe-Democrat*)

Allen J. Hubin, *The Bibliography of Crime Fiction, 1749-1975: Listing All Mystery, Detective, Suspense, Police and Gothic Fiction in Book Form Published in the English Language* (Del Mar: University Extension, University of California, San Diego, in Cooperation with Publisher's Inc., 1979, 697 pp.; $59.95)

    I almost didn't do this review, for it will take someone with a much greater knowledge of the field than I to do a real assessment of the degree of accuracy and comprehensiveness achieved. I've also had my copy for less than a week and have barely dipped into it here and there. Then I decided that it would be interesting to compare other reviews with my first impressions, so here they are.

    It is a large (29 cm.), attractively bound volume--maroon with silver lettering on the spine and front cover--with solid black endpapers. The binding is full cloth (not the cheap cloth-and-paper combination which Lippincott used for even the autographed editions of *Condominium*) and appears to be quite sturdy. The spine is fully glued to the signatures, yet supple enough to bend smoothly without cracking when the volume is fully opened. Ample margins were allowed and the pages lie flat without need for a weight. My only complaint with its physical appearance is the lack of a dust jacket. This is a truly disappointing omission. The text has been printed in three columns of varying depth, which produces a lot of white paper at the bottom of the pages. The printing appears to be photographically reduced typescript. It is small, but sharp, clean and quite legible.

    The contents consist of alphabetical author, title and series character indexes, plus Hubin's preface and introduction. The latter is short and succinct, explaining the organization of the work, Hubin's rationale for inclusions and exclusions, a bibliography of reference works consulted and acknowledgement of individuals who rendered assistance. (Nice to see so many familiar names there!) Hubin also announces here his intention to produce 5-year supplements, the first of which he is already at work on.

    The author index includes an author's real name (if known) and all known pseudonyms. Titles are listed under the name under which they first appeared. Publisher and date of first publication are given. If a work was published in both Britain and America, first publication date and publisher for both editions are given, as are any "reissue under altered byline or title, including any appearing *after 1975*...." (Emphasis added. Hubin does not give a cut-off date for post-1975 entries, but this cannot be later than the date of the introduction, November 2, 1978.) All known appearances of a series character are included. Short-story collections which contain at least one crim fiction story are included; anthologies are not. Short stories published separately, or under a variant title are identified, but full contents for short-story collections are not given. (That would be a project for someone!)

    No one could hope or pretend to produce a work of this magnitued without error or ommission, and Hubin readily acknowledges this. Correction of these will be a major function of the first supplement (1976-1980). (I think I've caught one. I found no listing for Ted Mark's *The Man from O.R.G.Y.* Didn't one or more of these appear before 1975?)

Nevertheless, this is an essential work for any serious reader, collector or student of the field of crime fiction. If Hubin doesn't win an award for such a truly substantial contribution, I'll lose what little respect I have left for the professional critics! (David H. Doerrer)

(continued from p. 18) and, I suspect, future. His Dr. Sam Hawthorne stories are an endangered species since they are actually detective short stories that play fair with the reader. "The Treasure of Jack the Ripper" in EQMM Oct. 1978 is the first story in that magazine about his detective Simon Ark who is allegedly 2,000 years old. To quote what is said about something else in this story, one wonders about Ark: Is he "...a hoax or a great historical discovery?"

In this story Ark functions as a jet-age Holmes, with the narrator his Watson. Ark calls on his "Watson" while the latter's wife is away, visiting her mother. They fly off to London. The story moves at a brisk pace and while its end is nto completely believable, Hoch deserves much credit for presenting such a fascinating "solution" to the Jack the Ripper case.

The "Golden Age" of the mystery short story ended when EQMM stopped its annual contest a little over twenty years ago. That magazine and its newly adopted brother publication, *Alfred Hitchcock's Mystery Magazine,* still provide consistent quality, even if their peaks are not as high as EQMM's once were. Furthermore, their publisher, Davis Publications 380 Lexington Ave. New York, N.Y. 10017 puts out impressive semi-annual anthologies based on their contents.

Ellery Queen's Anthology for Spring-Summer 1979 is not one of the best numbers, possibly because it relies too heavily on recent stories which by definition (my definition), are not as good as older EQMM material. Not surprisingly, I find the high point in the anthology to be Rex Stout's "The Fourth of July Picnic" (1958), one of the best of all Nero Wolfe novelets. At $2.25 for 21 stories, this is a bargain.

The Fall-Winter 1979 *Alfred Hitchcock* Anthology is an even bigger bargain with 29 stories and 352 pages for $2.50. There is at least one story for every year 1956 to 1973, and the list of authors reads like a current "who's who" of mystery short story writers: Robert Bloch, Henry Slesar, Donald Westlake, Jack Ritchie, Edward D. Hoch, Bill Pronzini, and Patricia Highsmith.

Variety is the spice of mystery fiction, and recently I read two novels as different as they can be. *Death Under Sail* (1932) is the first book, and only mystery, of Lord C. P. Snow, famous British novelist. It is an enjoyable, very old-fashioned book about murder aboard a yacht sailing the Norfolk Broads (which sounds like a British women's basketball team). The detective, Finbow, is an eccentric, Rex Harrison-type whose deductions are, unfortunately, not too convincing. Yet, the idea of murder in a closed setting still has its appeal.

Two years ago, using his own name, Timothy Welch published a paperback mystery, called *The Tennis Murders,* that is a literary footfault. It featured a hired detective-killer named Dion Quince. Late in 1978 Quince was back *(cont. p. 14)*

THE DOCUMENTS IN THE CASE
(Letters)

From Enola Stewart, Gravesend Books, Box 235, Pocono Pines, PA:
I came across this in my files and it brought to mind your
comments on it at an earlier time. [*Enola enclosed a photo-
stat of two printed pages, with a penciled notation in the
upper left-hand corner which reads "A [not legible]'s Eye
View of Punctuation Emerson Walling Summer 1962". What's the
missing word, Enola? Anyway, I will quote the pages in full,
since they are quite short.*]

    Worse than rivers, I think, are holes, especially those creat-
ed by periods and commas outside quotes. For example:
          He was a "hedonist". He enjoyed life.
What is that period doing over toward the beginning of the next
sentence? This is a practice common in England and becoming common in the United States.
    Here is a dilemma. Logically, if the quoted matter is intern-
al to the sentence the period should come outside the quotes, because the period is the point that ends everything, including all
parts of the sentence. But optically, the outside period looks
lost. Looks or logic--which? This dilemma is noticeable only
with the small points, the period and the comma. The tall points
look all right in the logical position:
          Was he a "hedonist"? He enjoyed life.
I have my definite choice. If I can not have both looks and
logic, I will take looks in this instance.
          He was a "hedonist." He enjoyed life.
People may not agree about the looks of the thing, granted. Yet
like it or not, the escaped period leaves a hole in the texture
of the text.

[*I lied; I'm leaving out a few sentences, since they don't
relate to the question. Now this fellow has got the right
idea regarding the logic of the matter, but he is way off
base otherwise. I don't trust myself to comment on his pre-
ference for looks over logic (I should have mentioned that
the type on the page is not set with justified margins, but
flows in and out, giving the page the look of an undulating
Coca-Cola bottle--looks over logic again, I suppose), but I
can't refrain from pointing out that, putting logic aside for
the moment, the quotation mark in the last instance ("hedonist.") looks even more out of place than does the period in
the first instance ("hedonist".). I contend that both looks
and logic demand a logical approach to the placement of quotation and punctuation marks, especially when the quotation
marks enclose a single word, or a title.*]
¶ No need for me to comment on Mr. Loeser's wide ranging
article for it should elicit enough mail for a decade of issues. However, I can state that his account of the New York
book store scene was quite accurate.

From Robert M. Williams, Box 242, Rule, TX 79547:
Guy, I wonder if you could give me any info. on the paperback
series--"The Saint Mystery Library". I am writing an aritcle
and any help would be greatly appreciated. There were at

least 14 books in the series beginning Aug. '59 with #118 (1) and ending with #131 (14). ¶ I need the title, author and contents for #119 (2) and #130 (13). ¶ I need the author and contents for #123 (6) "Murder in the Family & O.S." and #126 (9) "Executioner's Signature & O.S." I need the contents only for #120 (3) "Murder Set to Music & O.S." by Fredric Brown and #121 (4) "The Frightened Millionaire & O.S." by Craig Rice. (These question marks and periods are driving me crazy! I agree with you that the quotation marks should come before the period at the end of the sentence, but in this case where the period comes after the s, thereby abbreviating the word stories; I'm not sure. (Surely one does not add another period). [*The period which abbreviates also terminates, so there is no need for another one. Of course, if the quoted abbreviation ends an interrogatory sentence a question mark is used in addition to the period. Otherwise the following rule applies: whenever two punctuation marks occur at the same place in a sentence, the weaker is dropped entirely.*] ¶ I also need to know something about the publisher (Great American Pub. Inc), which seems to be closely aligned with Saint Publishing. [*Surely some of TMF's readers can--and will--supply you with the information you need.*]

From John Nieminski, 2948 Western, Park Forest, IL 60466: Hot flash! Have just obtained irrefutable proof from unimpeachable source that last 17 "Ellery Queen" books were in fact written by Francis Bacon. More details later, following my release. [*Or escape.*]

From Joe Lansdale, Rt. 8, Box 231, Nacogdoches, TX 75961: Thanks for correcting my correction of the letter I wrote for MF Vo.3 No. 1. The letter I sent last time was how I meant for it to read and was copied from the original draft, but when I typed it to send to you I must have made the boo-boo. Your correction did show originality. No matter. Ellen didn't send any money. ¶ Could you please list the controversial things in Bill Loeser's letter, please. Nothing really struck me as "fightin' words." [*Alas, Joe, I fear you have no soul.*] ¶ Thanks to Bob Briney for information concerning *Time and Again*. I'll watch for it. ¶ Joe Gall (spy fiction in general for that matter) is not a favorite of mine, but I enjoyed the chart by Jeff Banks and George Kelley. It might encourage me to try more Gall adventures. I did like *The Green Wound Contract* pretty well. ¶ . . . P.S. Enjoyed Steve's reviews best of all this time. His MYSTERY FILE is always a treat, but he outdid himself this time. Very fine. [*A later note:*] A short note of interest. Saw Sturgeon at AGGICON this past weekend, and in a filmed interview, he admitted to working on one of the Queen's, and said, "but out of respect to Manny we that have helped Ellery Queen don't mention it," words to that effect. Maybe Bill Crider, who was also there, can help me out on the exact statement. He also autographed a copy of *The Player on the Other Side*. Doesn't seem to be any mystery about that anymore. ¶ Sturgeon wrote at least that one Queen, and my guess is others from the jest of his conversation and the interview. I think its pretty common knowledge that Jack Vance did some of the books as well. ¶ Sturgeon spoke of the terrible writer's block that Manfred Lee had, one he never got over. Not trying to put a finger in the pie, I don't really care if Rasputin wrote the Queen books since they're not favorites of mine, but thought it might interest some completeist and Queen folks.

From Bill Crider, 4206 Ninth St., Brownwood, TX 76801: I'm not particularly fond of the works of Ellery Queen, and I really don't care who wrote all the books under that name, but I just have to tell what I know. At a science fiction convention recently, Theodore Sturgeon was interviewed by Lisa Tuttle. She asked him about the rumor that he'd written an Ellery Queen novel. He refused to answer with a yes or no. What he did say was that Manfred Lee had a terrible case of writer's block. He also said that since Lee was so well liked, those who "helped out" didn't like to talk about it. What he seemed to imply was that Lee was "blocked" for quite some time and that there were a number of people who had a hand in the books. And he didn't *deny* having written a Queen book. ¶ For those who don't believe me, or who don't trust my inferences, I can offer no corroboration. Joe R. Lansdale, a reader of TMF was also in attendance, however, and you can ask him what he thought. ¶ Now I'll descend to the Kiwanis Club Banquet mode and say that George Kelley did a really good job on Joe Gall, and Jeff's chart was great (not to mention David's typing). As for your new staff curmudgeon, I would have thought that one curmudgeon would have been enough; but as long as you felt the need for someone to keep you company, I suppose Mr. Loeser will do. He certainly has some interesting opinions (not necessarily facts) about the academic world. Or maybe he just knows something I don't.

From Jon Breen, 10642 La Bahia Ave., Fountain Valley, CA: Some random comments on the latest fine issue of TMF: I don't object to a critic's revealing the solution to a detective novel if such a revelation is necessary to make a point. What I *do* object to is giving away the solution for *no good reason,* which is usually the way it happens. Mr. Loeser could easily have made his point in your lead article without giving away any solutions. Wile I will agree that it is virtually impossible for anyone sufficiently immersed in mystery fiction to be reading TMF *not* to know the surprise solution of *The Murder of Roger Ackroyd,* I submit that such is *not* the case with John Dickson Carr's *Death Turns the Tables,* of which Mr. Loeser also blows the secret. (Another place where the Ackroyd secret is gratuitously given away is in the opening pages of Kathleen Tynan's *Agatha,* which conceivably *could* have had some readers who didn't know the solution.) ¶ Let's see now--what else did Mr. Loeser say that made me mad? I think calling *Royal Bloodline* a work of "hagiography" is an inaccurate slur. While it's true that Mike Nevins didn't delve into the authorship of the EQ paperbacks and juveniles, he pretty effectively identified them as ersatz Queen by not discussing them in the book. As for the adult hard-cover novels about Ellery Queen the *character* (and the one pb original, *A Study in Terror*), I don't think anyone has claimed that Dannay and Lee were not involved in the writing of them, even if a third collaborator might have been brought in on occasion. ¶ Oddly enough, I vividly remember Carolyn Wells' *The Tannahill Tangle* for a reason completely different from

Mr. Loeser's. The clue to the killer in that book is one of the wackiest and most unforgettable in detective fiction. If I were feeling self-indulgent, I would tell you what it was. I agree that this is probably one of the worst detective novels of the Golden Age (though Wells *did* write some good ones) and therefore I think everyone should read it. Anyone who identified with Bill Proncini's TAD article about the Phoenix Press will understand my statement. ¶ The young Orson Welles as Archie Goodwin? Can't buy it. My own choice for Archie is George Peppard, though I guess he's a little old for the part now. ¶ On the theory that a good book review should give the flavor of a book, Perry Dillon's review of Edmund Crispin's *The Glimpses of the Moon* is an excellent one. If I had not read the book already, Mr. Dillon's review would have convinced me that I would enjoy it, even though the reviewer didn't like it at all. (Though I value Crispin's style and humor more than Mr. Dillon does, it's quite true the book is not distinguished as a fair play mystery, which Crispin's earlier novels usually were.)

From John Harwood, 142A Highland Ave., N. Dartmouth, MA 02747: Randy Cox doesn't think the idea of the charts of series books is a good idea because it will "merely emphasize the formula and mechanical aspects of the books and does not really contribute to an appreciation of what the authors have done." ¶ He also said that someone told him one time that such a chart gives away the villains. This may be true in most cases where there is an actual mystery where the villain isn't revealed until the end of the book. ¶ On the other hand, as Mr. Cox says, it doesn't matter in the case of thrillers as you know the identity of the villain from the first. For instance, you know who the villain is in Sax Rohmer's Fu Manchu and Sumuru books and Ian Fleming's James Bond books. ¶ I hadn't realized that there was any doubt who wrote some of the earlier Saint books. I knew, of course, that the later ones were written by other authors for the TV program and were then published in book form with Leslie Charteris' permission (and the payment of a royalty). ¶ That there is a belief that some of the previous ones had been ghosted is news to me. ¶ I have been reading the Saint books for years since *The Last Hero* was published. In addition I've also read all the non-Saint books, with the exception of *The Bandit*. ¶ Gary Crew liked the suggestion from a letter in one of your earlier issues regarding an article on juvenile mystery fiction. I, too, used to read the Hardy Boys series by Franklin W. Dixon. Years later, I used to give the little girl next door copies of the Nancy Drew books for Christmas and birthday presents. Each year she would give me a list of the titles she hadn't read and I would pick out one for the special event. ¶ These series of juvenile mysteries were written by Edward L. Stratemeyer who also wrote many other series like The Bobbsey Twins, Tom Swift, Don Sturdy, Bomba, the Jungle Boy, the X-Bar-X Boys, the Rover Boys, and many other series. ¶ Originally Stratemeyer wrote all his own books. Then in the early years of this century he turned to the assembly line method of writing books. He would start up a new series and write the first few books in the series. Then he would write outlines for the rest of the titles and have hack writers fill in the outlines to book length. ¶

While this was going on, he would write the first few books of a new series. Then he would turn this new series over to other writers and go on to start still another series. In this way, he was responsible for almost a thousand books, if not more. [*Don't stop there, John; how about an article from you on the subject?*]

From Carl Larsen, 3872 Amboy Road, Staten Island, NY 10308: By the way, although I have avoided almost all the recent Holmes revival, even giving my deerstalker to one of my children, I did see and enjoy the film called Murder By Decree-- another rip-off of the Ripper--with some what I thought were superb background and period detail. And James Mason as a Watson to remember. It was a bit too long and sentimental, but I thoroughly enjoyed it. I went expecting another unfaithful version--I couldn't abide the *Seven Percent* and all the other recently discovered manuscripts. The fact must be that to write like Doyle, one has to have been born when the world moved at a more leisurely pace and one had a clearer vision of what good and evil meant, as well as what was good prose and what was not. P.G. Wodehouse could write very like Doyle: the marvelous way of announcing some "profound" statement in a memorable way. I think Wodehouse and Doyle both were bigger than what they were doing and, in aiming at entertainment, hit art as well. The pastichers are over their heads when it comes to prose and rely on established characters and garish, unlikely plots. [*I rejoice whenever I find someone else with the proper appreciation for Wodehouse. One of my greatest regrets is that I put off writing a fan letter to him until it was too late. He gave joy.*]

From Ellen Nehr, 207 S. Cassady Rd., Bexley, Ohio 43209: I can't stand it! The withdrawal symptoms are horrible; my fingers itch, I've bruised a toe kicking the typewriter. I crave the taste of the glue on an envelope flap, and I can't pass the post office without going in and making a duty call. Disregard my last letter about retiring to *Mrs*. Annonymous category. If I exercise judicious selection among the letters and articles I might be able to describe activities in this Elba of Ohio well enough to incite activity among your subscribers in their home towns which, in turn, will add immearurely to their prestige, circle of acquaintences and, perhaps indirectly, to your list of readers, and keep me out of trouble. ¶ The Bexley library has a collection of perhaps 5,000 old and older mystery books, mostly rebound, since their original covers were worn out. I suggested to the person in charge of the window display cases that such assets should be flaunted and was given carte-blanche to "Do it yourself", which I will next month. Rather than pull some of their copies from circulation I'm going to lend a few things from my shelves, with the Murder Ink butler cover as an eye catcher, flanked by Mystery FANcier and Poisoned Pen. Several of the book jackets, which I own, are in quite good condition for their age, and one of Phoebe Atwood Taylor's has a photo of Asey Mayo on the back. I'll throw in a Dell Map-Back or two, a DAPA-EM Sherlocian cover (to provide equal space), a Nancy Drew to bring back memories and Encyclopedia Brown for balance. The time to prepare all of this is minimal, cost is nil, and the rewards are immeasurable. I may even go as far as allowing my copy of that glorious Hubin Bibliography of Crime Fiction 1749-1975 out of my hands. If it only had been given a proper (or even improper) dust jacket by its short sighted publishers I wouldn't have to use the 'butler' as a centerpiece. Brownish-red burlap is not that appealing. ¶ Recently, The Friends Of The Ohio State University Library sponsored a FREE series of lectures, discussions and activities about Book Collecting. They were held in various rooms in the Student Union, each place different, since the group kep over-flowing the space allotted to it. Their ulterior purpose, of course, was to get new members, and I did learn a bit more about Americana than I wanted to know but, what a marvelous way to meet new people, exchange ideas and, best of all, find out names and addresses of book shops in outlying towns. They are going to do it again next fall with a different cast. Again, this project didn't cost a thing, except time and interest and a few dollars spent for the coffee served at the end. ¶ Randy Cox said "Mystery fans .....live in a world apart and speak little to mortals", well, here is a chance to find your own Olympus.

From David Doerrer, 4626 Baywood Circle, Pensacola, FL 32504: An interesting article by Bakerman on Gene Stratton-Porter, though I don't think I'll look up the books; too many other things I want to read. The Len Deighton chart was more to my taste. His *SS-GB* has gotten a couple of good reviews so far. A nice, concise article on the books about Philby. Don Yates report on Bouchercon nicely complimented Mary Ann's, and the photos weren't that bad. They have a taken-by-agent-under-adverse-circumstances look which appealed to me. ¶ By now everyone must know about my fondness for letter columns, so it is really redundant for me to tell you how much I enjoyed those in 3:1, not the least for seeing my name mentioned. I thought it showed remarkable forebearance on your part not to insert a (sic) after my inexcusable misspelling of Nacogdoches. I will be most interested in Jean-Jacques Schleret's article if it appears in an English translation. I can cope with foreign language quotations, but a whole article is something else. I'm glad that Jeff Banks liked my listing of the contributors to *Murder Ink*, but it really wasn't all that much work. What I belatedly thought I should have done, for the benefit of other neophytes, was to identify all those pseudonyms which someone said Dilys Winn used. Joe Lansdale expressed one of the best arguments for letter columns: many of us *will* write a letter when we won't, for whatever reason, attempt a review or article. Jon Breen's remarks, and yours, on Thayer David finally triggered an illusive memory. Didn't David play Dragon in the movie version of *The Eiger Sanction*? [*Yep.*] If I'm right, then I can't see him as Nero Wolfe. As James Munro's Loomis maybe, but not Wolfe. ¶ That has to be it for 3:1. I'm so far behind that I've even put a couple of book lists aside, which is a good way to get nothing! I won't dwell on the cover typos, but I didn't want you to think that I read it so carelessly that I didn't notice them! [*Another letter:*] At the risk of getting on the wrong side of that rock-throwing line, or otherwise incurring your awesome wrath [*I'm glad someone has an appreciation of my vast powers.*], I have to say I side with William R. Loeser on the subject of revealing who, why or what did it in a critical discussion of mystery fiction. Note that I say "critical discussion". Loeser distinguishes between reviewing and criticism, as I did in a mailing comment to Dorothy Nathin in *For Your Eyes Only*, 79-2:07. I think it's a valid distinction, and further agree with his statement that the freedom to reveal villain, plot, etc., should not extend to recently published works. If this prohibition against revelation is rigorously adhered to for all titles out of deference to those who haven't yet read them, how will we ever get any critical analysis of an author's works? Very few of us will ever read all the titles in Hubin's bibliography, let alone those which will be published in the future. Must this forever inhibit discussion? Let an author/editor give the reader fair warning that who, what and why will be discussed (as you did on the Bakerman article on P.D. James in TMF 1:5) and those readers for whom the stories would be spoiled can postpone the critical discussion until they have read the works themselves. (I know that sounds inconsistent with what I said above about "recently published works". What I meant to type was "should not extend to *reviews of* . . . .", but I'm not going to type this over! You can insert those two words, if this gets published, and save yourself copying this whole sentence.) [*I could, that is, had I read your letter over again before I typed it up. As it is, I'm damned if I'm going to type this over!* ¶ *This is as good a time as any, I suppose, to insert my two-cents-worth on this subject. I had read many, many hundreds of mysteries before I ever heard of Roger Ackroyd. His name was first mentioned to me by the chairman of my dissertation committee, who happened to know of my interest in mysteries. I remember the incident well. It was at one of those enjoyable but at the same time faintly uncomfortable parties where faculty and graduate students get together and try to show each other that they are humans too. Anyway, we were discussing mysteries in general and he asked if I had read* The Murder of Roger Ackroyd. *When I replied that I had not he refused to discuss it any further, saying that he would not spoil the delightful surprise for me. Of course, that only whetted my appetite for the book, and sure enough when I did read it I immediately placed it high on my list of favorite mysteries, and it has remained there ever since. Had he told me the secret, much of the delight of reading the book would have been destroyed. As for the idea that everyone reading TMF has probably already read* Roger, *put forth earlier in this letter column, I think the assumption is a bit shakey. I have read thousands of mysteries, but there are still many, many excellent ones, and old ones at that, that I haven't read, and to assume that just because I read this magazine I am aware of all the significant plots --even the outstanding ones--is to err significantly. Even identifying articles and reviews which discuss whodunit and how and asking those unfamiliar with the author to stay away has its drawbacks. You mention Jane's James article, David, so let's look at it. It is a splendid discussion of a very significant author, and could lead many mystery readers not yet familiar with James's work to read her. But the warning that certain things were given away in the article may have kept someone from reading the article, and that someone may never acquire the interest in James which the article would have engendered, and may therefore never read any of James's* excellent works. There is no easy, completely satisfactory solution. The best we can hope for, it seems to me, is to avoid, whenever it is possible without defeating the purpose of an article, giving away anything which will detract from the first-time reader's enjoyment if known beforehand. Subscribers to this magazine, I honestly believe, are of better than average intelligence, and can use their intelligence to write their letters and articles and reviews in such a way as not to spoil anyone else's fun. I don't say that whodunit and how and why should never been revealed--otherwise there could never be articles on such subjects as outstanding locked-room murder devices, and such--but I do believe that more often than not such revelations are unnecessary and result from laziness or childish perversity. I remember, to my everlasting shame, telling an undergraduate classmate of mine what the last sentence in 1984 is. Of course, it ruined the book for him, and I've felt guilty about it ever since.] ¶ Having agreed with Loeser, I'll now proceed to disagree. I don't think that Martin Wooster needs defending, at least not on the grounds Loeser uses. As I recall the Wooster et al exchanges, most of his critics objected less to what he said than the manner in which he said it. The most notable exception was Martin's choice of verbe in saying that he had "proved" that Queen had not written at least one of the stories, based on no more than a casual conversation with Theodore Sturgeon. I jumped on Martin for this, as did others. Martin's response, if my memory is correct without looking it up, was that he was leaving it up to others to provide the "proof" of this statement. Well, I don't agree with that either, but I don't think that this is what Loeser is defending; at least I hope it isn't. ¶ While on the subject, more or less, of *The Player on the Other Side,* The following appeared in a letter from Gary McDone, on page 195 of TAD 10:3: "In Marvel Comics black & white magazine *Unknown Worlds of Science Fiction* (Vol. 1, 1976, p. 18) there is an interview with the well-known science fiction writer Theodore Sturgeon. The introduction to this article mentions 'His ghost-authored "Ellery Queen' novel, *The Player on the Other Side.'* Could you (or any TAD reader) tell me if this is a) misinformation, b) a casually dropped bombshell, c) something knowledgeable people knew all along, or d) none of the above?" ¶ Now, unless my memory is terribly defective (and I'm sure someone will tell me if it is), McDole has done essentially the same thing that Wooster did, i.e. pass on an item of (apparently) controversial nature on a second-hand basis. (I'm not going to debate whether an introduction by an unnamed person to an interview is more or less "authoritative" than a reported statement by the same person, the interviewee.) Did McDole's letter raise the same storm as Wooster's? Apparently not. I, unfortunately, don't have a complete backfile of TAD readily available and thus could not check the letters in 10:4 for a response to McDole, but 11:1 which contains several letters referring to various items in 10:3, produced no howls of wrath. My point here is that I feel the non-response to McDole's letter supports my contention that Martin has been criticized more for his acerbic tone than for his content. In short, Loeser's defense is misplaced in that it at least appears to defend an aspect of Martin's writing which had not been attacked. . . . ¶ Loeser makes some tell-

ing points in his analysis of the Scylla and Charybdis of
mystery fiction journals, but I think he overstates the dire
straits of both TAD and TMF. I could be wrong; my perceptions
are based on a bare two year's acquaintance with both. Has
anyone ever looked at the statud of the "academic" contributors to TAD? Are they primarily young, insecure, untenured,
or vice versa? What I presume he is objecting to in TMF is
the content of the letter column, or at least a portion there-
of. If so, O.K. I accept, albeit sadly, that there are some
of us who don't like letter columns. Fine. Don't read them!
That still leaves an average 5/6 of an issue composed of articles and reviews, unless Loeser includes favorable reviews
as a form of complimenting others. Of course, I may be missing his point, or too dense to see what he has seen, but if
he really is objecting to letter columns, then he should say
so; others have. Rats! He did say so, quite plainly. I
should stop typing these letters when I get excited about
something, or else be willing to re-type when I commit such
a sloppy error! I'm still too dense, however, to detect his
symptoms in the articles. ¶ Since he doesn't like compli-
ments on contributions, I'll refrain from saying anything
about how interesting his descriptions of New York City bookstores were, or about how valuable they are to neophytes in
the NYC area. I'll just gripe about his directions. What is
this SE, SW, E side N of 87th St.? I operate on right, left,
up, down, forward or back, and anyone who wants me to do
otherwise had better be prepared for an absolute non-response.
¶ His reviews emphasize the point made later on by Randy Cox
in his letter. Should reviews which are not included in the
reviews section be indexed? I should have asked you this
question last year before I did the index. I can easily include them in this year's, as well as going back and doing a
supplement for Vols. 1 & 2. [*I have never met a more dedi-
cated masochist; you're on.*] ¶ After re-reading the above,
I guess you may refer to me as "The Curmudgeon in the Other
Corner". It also illustrates the fact that I react with more
vigor than I act. You comment in the editorial that Martin
Wooster seems to have taken his marbles and left. I hope
not. I also hope that I don't in any way contribute to driving William Loeser away. We need someone (other than our
"sweetness-and-light" editor) to stir the troops up occasion-
ally. ¶ On the balance of the issue, my apologies for the
tight edge-of-page margins on the Joe Gall Chart. I'll watch
the next one more closely. What happened to the page numbers? Most of them don't seem to be there. [*They were there
but the folks who made my masters chopped them off. What
have I done to deserve this constant grief with the print-
ers?*] Glad to see Marvin Lachman back, with a slightly longer than usual column. ¶ Almost forgot one typo that bothers
me. In quoting from Jeff Banks' postcard, you have " . . .
anecdote from *Suitable for Hanging* . . .". Jeff's text on
the copy I typed from (and Hubin's *Bibliography*) give the
title as *Suitable for Framing*. You know I don't (usually)
nit-pick typos, but that one might send some deluded soul off
looking for a non-existent title. [*That's not the sort of
typo that I usually make, but since I can't lay my hands on
Jeff's postcard at the moment, I'll go ahead and accept full
blame. You are quite right--looking for a non-existent
title is no fun.*] ¶ What can I say about the Saga and the

letters, without offending Loeser that is? Speaking of erudition, what gives with Gary Crew and his Junior or Senior von Nagyrapolt's? Obviously another one of my heavy-handed attempts at humor fell flat on its sore little face. I was looking for a complex name and pulled that one out of the "Biographical Names" section of my *Webster's New Collegiate*. Trust TMF to have a reader familiar with a "Hung. chem." Now I know how John Nieminski felt with that precocious teen ager at Bouchercon. Also serves me right for pulling Ellen's leg over Nacogdoches. There is a special place reserved you-know-where for people like Bob Briney who tell us about bookstores like Kilnapps *after* they're gone. On the other hand, anyone who has the same feelings towards words like "herstory" that I do has to have his heart in the right place. Have you seen the proposal to change "hurricane" to "himicane"? John Nieminski is right about the libbers. A special welcome back to Sandy Sandulo. Her letters have a special something about them that our more sober-sided, world-weary senior fans should take note of. We aren't all bored and/or exasperated experts thirsting for purely relevant factual material. ¶ End of this issue's epistle. Have I raised enough hackles?

From Jane Gottschalk, 611 A Franklin, Oshkosh, WI 54901: The double issues of 3:2 were both entertainingly informative, with something for everyone in the essays or in the documents in the case. You must have anticipated flying fur and feathers, so here's a pinfeather:

> For William C. Loeser
>
> There was a curmudgeon named Bill
> Who of others thought nothing but ill.
>   In his rant and his rail
>   There's no logical nail:
> Ad hominem argument--nil.
>
> He throws casual assumptions like dice,
> And that's naughty and not a bit nice.
>   He should footnote his "data"
>   Like a good old Phi Beta.
> An asterisk does not suffice.

If this is too dull, he might note:

> Little Boy Bill
> His blown his horn;
> The scholars are writing
> But them he does scorn.
>
> Where, oh, where
> Is Little Boy Bill?
> Checking out bookstores
> In a weep.

From Marvin Lachman, 34 Yorkshire Drive, Suffern, NY 10901: I received and enjoyed the *real* March-April 1979 issue. Who is William R. Loeser, and why is he saying those things about me--and everyone else. Actually, he is right on most issues, and I'm glad to see him introduce some more lively controversy into TMF. Regarding giving away the identity of the murderer, Mr. Loeser raises critical discussion above preserving the element of surprise and suspense. I'm afraid that is putting the cart before the horse. However, it is possible to eat your cake and have it too if the reviewer* will do what I suggested--warning the reader in advance that the criminal or surprise plot device will be discussed. ¶ I still haven't figured out the following in the letter from Sandy Sandulo: "Maybe a picture of Marvin Lachman so I can decide why he seems cross w/me when I read him." I'm not cross with people who read me--only with people who don't Seriously, I didn't think my columns and articles sounded mean. My wife doesn't think they sound mean. ¶ Trust Jon Breen, about the best mystery reviewer abound these days, to bring some sanity to the question of authorship of the Queen paperbacks. *Death Spins the Platter* (1962), *Wife or Death* (1963) and *Blow Hot, Blow Cold* (1964) are good books, better than most of the Queen hardcovers of the Sixties, no matter who wrote them. (*Or critic.)

From Bob Adey, 7 Highcroft Ave., Wordsley, Stourbridge, West Midlands, DY8 5LX, England: [*I have written letters shorter than Bob's address.*] I am fairly certain that in an earlier issue of TMF I gave readers some information on the locked room biblio that I hoped to get published and I think it's only fair (and a bit of publicity of course) if I give an update on the situation for those who may be interested and don't already know from other sources. The biblio has been pasted up by my long suffering editor and is with the printer. He says that it should be ready some time in May, though initial estimates that it would be the beginning of that month have now shifted to the end of the month. The cost will be ₤8 and the publisher is Ferret Fantasy of London. Some day I'll write an article for somebody [*Me, maybe?*] on how difficult and long winded it is to get this sort of work published. It really is quite surprising. ¶ May I pass on to fellow readers a little bit of information that has probably eluded many of them. Glynn Carr is highly thought of for his detective fiction with its mountaineering flavour and his likeable detective, Abercrombie Lewker. It is no great secret that Carr is a pseudonym for the main stream novelist, Showell Styles, or even that one or two early titles under Styles' own name were criminous. However when I recently bought a copy of one of these early Styles titles I was amazed to find that not only was it a full fledged thriller, but that the detective-hero was none other than our old friend (except that he was a lot younger then) Lewker! The book concerned is Kidnap Castle published by Selwyn and Blount in 1947 and the blurb points out that it is our old friends who first appeared in the even earlier book, Traitor's Mountain (Selwyn 1946). Another book, Hammer Island is also mentioned among the "latest fiction" while the TAD biblio rewrite lists yet another, Dark Hazard, also from Selwyn. Could it be that there are not two, but four or more, lost Lewkers? Or am I passing on information that is already common knowledge? Very few examples can I think of of authors who have changed their pen name and taken their detective with them when they did so. In fact off hand I can think of only one other, Hugo Blayn (John Russell Fearn) whose Inspector Garth stayed with him for his last book under the Nat Karta pseudonym. (Unless you count Anthony Berkeley whose first Roger Sheringham novel was published in the U.K. anonymously.)

From Dick Moskowitz, 110 Dunrovin Lane, Rochester, NY 14618: As one of the original subscribers to TMF and having read the latest issue, I wonder what the Fancier has become and in which direction it is headed. Our esteemed publisher and editor must surely recognize that something is drastically wrong. In fact, there are several things needing correction. Let me cover this area before dissecting one William R. Loeser. ¶ In the preview issues of November 1976, Guy Townsend tells his future subscribers that it is his intent to create a general mystery fanzine consisting of a balance of articles. reviews and letters. Well, I submit, Mr. Townsend, that you have strayed from your goals. ¶ From its inception, TMF has been beset with basic problems. One of the first was printing and format. Surely, the changes of format, type-size changes, readability, and the change from mimeograph to offset to the present and more readable printing have been disconcerting to say the least. How many subscribers have fallen by the wayside by receiving undecipherable copies? [*None, I trust, since I have never knowingly sent out an undecipherable copy.*] How many actually were lost by the change from a yearly subscription basis of $7.50 to $9.00? I doubt that many were affected; that's not even the cost of a healthy sandwich these days and for the dollar-and-a-half difference there is a full year's reading pleasure to be obtained. Where can one buy good paperbacks for $1.50 these days? Surely there is some attrition due to loss of interest in the mystery genre, but most of the subscription loss has to be accounted for by the other problems. The last of what I consider to be the basis problems is in the direction TMF is taking, and it is headed towards academia. [*Gasp!*] ¶ Now, please don't take me wrong. I am not against academics or writing dissertations. I do not discourage the teachers in our midst, and there are several, who write letters and enjoyable ones at that. Their letters, however, should be addressed to the subscribers who make up the mailings of the Fancier. I wonder how many of us have the pleasure, as I have, of receiving letters from various subscribers? The myst ery genre has been the beginnings of friendship and correspondence with many of you. In some cases, this has led to phone calls between us, and in the future it will lead to meetings in person. Isn't that what a fanzine intends to accomplish along the way? But the question remains, has TMF lost its direction? ¶ An example in point. The Curmudgeon in the Corner by William R. Loeser. Now I don't have the foggiest as to who he really is, or what his credentials pretend to be, but I think some of his comments should be directed to TAD or elsewhere. I will grant you that he is well read. I will grant you that he appears knowledgeable. And I assure you that he has been reading and remembering mysteries long before I became interested. I will not put the "knock" on him as a person. But who is this man who claims one author rightly takes to task another author? Who is this man to tell me that I must read Trent's last case or The Murder of Roger Ackroyd or The Crooked Hinge before reading the

Mystery Fancier or my priorities are on backwards? I wonder
Mr. Loeser if you have ever heard of people. I get the impression that you could not write anything with the characters dealt with in depth. And since this is a Fanzine with a capital "F", which of us does have his priorities reversed?
¶ If, perhaps, The Mystery Fancier is fulfilling the need for people to communicate with one another, just what, Mr. Loeser, is so terribly wrong? Does discussion of the mystery genre lack for it in the pages of TMF? I seriously doubt it. It would appear to me as a declared novice in the field that you are paying your money for both, and I repeat that, bot for discussion of mysteries and for the communication with others having similar interests. ¶ I will now thank you for your interesting article as pertaining to the book stores of New York. Having lived there, surely you know wherein you speak. I will also thank you in advance for your projected and forthcoming article on sales of mysteries by mail; and to the many booksellers who have helped me to over-fill my library, I give thanks to them also, even though my fair city is not really a hick-town when it comes to rare and antiquarian mysteries--it just seems that way. I could go on, but our editor/publisher neglected to number the pages. ¶ To Mr. Loeser, even your reviews and critiques will not discourage me from reading the books you mention or the plots you tried to give away or in fact did give away. I'm afraid that if that was your intention you lose. ¶ But, let's get back to Mr. Townsend. Since The Mystery Fancier has lost fifty per cent of its subscribers by your own account, Guy, its time now to take stock of the situation. Although most things in life are not really free, I offer a free suggestion to you. Only the carrying out of the idea will cost you money. ¶ It is my contention that the editor should send a letter to all living former subscribers and include a survey to determine why these people are no longer with us. The total monetary cost would be fifteen cents per letter and ten cents each for the survey cards. I believe the answers would amaze you --and I believe that I have saved you $25.00 by telling you what the former subscribers would give for their answers. ¶ TMF might very well gain by what the former subscribers reply. Printing, format changes, the change to academic writing all must bear some responsibility. ¶ Let's keep the mystery in TMF within its pages. Let's solve the mystery of TMF's growth and do it now while there is still time! [*Prior to receiving Dick's letter I did write to all former subscribers to remind them that their subs had lapsed. Partly as a result of this, subscriptions now approach the 200 mark. As for the question, Whither TMF?--I am delighted with the way TMF has improved from issue to issue. The letters and reviews have always been good, and the articles are getting better with each issue. There is, among these articles, a mixture of Gee Whiz articles and scholarly articles, which is the way I like it. And I have no intention of changing it so long as I can get the kinds of contributions I have gotten to date. TMF is a damned fine fanzine, and you should all be proud of it; I know I am.*]

www.ingramcontent.com/pod-product-compliance
Lightning Source LLC
Chambersburg PA
CBHW031427040426
42444CB00006B/714